Some Notable
Surveyors & Map-Makers of the
Sixteenth, Seventeenth, & Eighteenth
Centuries and their Work

The *Armorial Bearings of* CHRISTOPHER SAXTON, *of
Dunningley in the County of York, Gentleman, Granted by*
WILLIAM FLOWER, NORROY, 1 *July* 1579,
as recorded at the College of Arms, 1927

Some Notable Surveyors & Map-Makers of the Sixteenth, Seventeenth, & Eighteenth Centuries and their Work

A Study in the History of Cartography

by

SIR HERBERT GEORGE FORDHAM

Author of *Hertfordshire Maps: A Descriptive Catalogue of the Maps of the County, 1579–1900*; *The Cartography of the Provinces of France, 1570–1757*; *Studies in Carto-Bibliography*; *Catalogue des Guides-Routiers et des Itinéraires Français, 1552–1850*; *Maps: Their History, Characteristics and Uses*; *The Road-Books and Itineraries of Great Britain, 1570–1850*; *John Cary, Engraver, Map, Chart and Print-Seller and Globe-Maker*, and other works

CAMBRIDGE

AT THE UNIVERSITY PRESS

1929

CAMBRIDGE
UNIVERSITY PRESS

University Printing House, Cambridge CB2 8BS, United Kingdom

Cambridge University Press is part of the University of Cambridge.

It furthers the University's mission by disseminating knowledge in the pursuit of education, learning and research at the highest international levels of excellence.

www.cambridge.org
Information on this title: www.cambridge.org/9781107452855

© Cambridge University Press 1929

First published 1929
First paperback edition 2014

A catalogue record for this publication is available from the British Library

ISBN 978-1-107-45285-5 Paperback

PREFACE

THIS little book is, as will be gathered from the title, an attempt to bring into something of narrative form, associated with the personality of some one notable individual, or family, in each case, an outline of the development and progress of the art and science of cartography during the long period which precedes the modern systematic surveys organized by the Governments of the countries of Europe and the American Continent.

The study is not a complete and exhaustive one, inasmuch as it does not deal with the immense cartographical output of the Dutch and Flemish School of map-makers of the sixteenth and seventeenth centuries, nor with the maps produced in the former century in Italy, and at most it only claims to be a sketch.

But, with these recognized omissions, there remains a sufficient historical sequence and continuity to justify my title and the ideas it represents.

I have first dealt with the remarkable work of survey carried out in the reign of Queen Elizabeth by Christopher Saxton and with its development, and with its influence on cartography in the British Isles through at least a century. This work may well be regarded as laying the foundation of the conception of modern cartography.

In the next century I have selected the famous French cartographer Nicolas Sanson, whose maps, as a whole, present a typical example of definite progress in the science to which he devoted his life, and whose work was further developed by his sons and successors; his influence in French and World cartography extending until nearly the middle of the eighteenth century.

The foundation of exact and scientific survey at the hands of successive members of the Cassini family and their associates may be said to fill the eighteenth century with the triangulation and mapping of France, leading up to the elaborate mapping of the roads of France, and finally to our own Ordnance Survey and to the remarkable " Regional Survey" and map of the Austrian Provinces of the Low Countries undertaken by the Comte de Ferraris.

Some reference to a typical English cartographer, John Cary, who flourished in the latter part of the eighteenth and the beginning of the nineteenth century, and to General William Roy and the preliminary work from which sprang, at the end of the former century, the British and Irish Government surveys and mapping, brings me to the point of time and of cartographical progress which I indicated above as having been selected as the limit of this work.

It will be found, I hope, to contain a large amount of historical information useful for obtaining an idea of the magnitude and character of the long, continuous labour necessary for the building up of cartography as a science of world extension and fundamental to geography itself, and leading to something of a distant personal acquaintance with the men, their lives, and their devotion to the work they have so happily advanced to a final success in the now stereotyped form of survey and of map delineation.

A list of Works of Reference has been added, in order that materials may be at the service of students, for following up, without undue loss of time, the facts upon which the sketch here offered is based. An Index is also supplied.

H. G. F.

ODSEY
October 1st 1928

CONTENTS

CHAP.   PAGE

I. The Elizabethan Surveyors, their Work, and its Influence on the British Cartography of the Seventeenth Century

    I. Christopher Saxton, Philip Lea, and the Quartermaster's Map . .   1

    II. John Norden, Philip Symonson, and Estate Surveys   9

    III. The County Maps of England and Wales of the Seventeenth Century   15

    IV. The Art and Technique and General History of the Cartography of the Sixteenth and Seventeenth Centuries   18

II. The French School of Cartography of the Seventeenth Century

    I. Nicolas Sanson and his Engravers and Publishers   23

    II. The Younger Sansons and the Jaillot Family of Cartographers .   .   29

    III. The Art of the French School of the Seventeenth Century and its Relations with the Cartography of the following Century .   .   .   35

CHAP.   PAGE

III. Cartography as an Exact Science. Its Development in the Eighteenth Century in
France

      I. The Cassini Family and the Triangula-
tion and Mapping of France   .   39

     II. The Cartographical Work of the
French Road Surveyors of the
Eighteenth Century   .   .   . 57

    III. The Map of the Belgian Provinces of
the Comte de Ferraris .   .   . 62

IV. British Cartography of the Second Half of
the Eighteenth Century, its Connection
with the Triangulation of France, and the
Ordnance Survey

      I. John Cary and his Work .   .   68

     II. General William Roy and the Early
History of the Ordnance Survey . 76

Conclusion 86

List of Works of Reference 88

Index 93

LIST OF ILLUSTRATIONS

I. ARMS OF CHRISTOPHER SAXTON,   FRONTISPIECE
of Dunningley, as granted 1 July, 1579, and now
re-drawn and recorded at the College of Arms,
7 January, 1927

PAGE

II. WALDSEEMÜLLER'S *POLYMETRUM* .   .   .   4
slightly reduced from the plate in the *Margarita
Philosophica Nova* of Gregorius Reisch, edition
of 1512. Argentine [Strasburg], 1512. 4⁰.

III. MAP OF THE DISTRICT OF NORTHAMPTONSHIRE,   17
Bedfordshire, Cambridgeshire, Huntingdonshire
and Rutlandshire, engraved by Pieter van den
Keere (*Petrus Kaerius*) in 1599, after Christopher
Saxton's map of 1576. From the Latin epitome
of Camden's *Britannia*, published by Regnerus
Vitellius. Amsterdam, 1617. 12⁰.

IV. SECTION FROM MAP BY NICOLAS SANSON   .   25
(engraved by R. Cordier) of the *Anciens Royaumes
de Mercie et East-Angles*, 1654. From the atlas,
the *Cartes Générales de Toutes les Parties du
Monde*. Paris, 1658. Fol.

V. PORTRAIT OF ALEXIS HUBERT JAILLOT   .   .   29
géographe du roi (1632–1712). Reduced from that
of the frontispiece of the *Atlas Nouveau*. Paris,
1698. Large fol.

VI. SECTION FROM THE *NOUVELLE CARTE*   .   .   45
qui comprend les principaux *Triangles qui servent
de Fondement à la Description Géométrique de la
France*. J. D. Maraldi and C. F. Cassini de
Thury. 1744.

PAGE

VII. SECTION FROM SHEET 2 (COMPIÈGNE, ETC.) .   51
     published in 1756, of the map of France in 182
     sheets, by Maraldi and Cassini de Thury.

VIII. TITLE-PAGE OF *CARY'S ACTUAL SURVEY*   .   68
      *of the Great Post Roads between London and
      Falmouth, including a Branch to Weymouth.*
      London, 1784. 12º.

IX. SOUTH-EAST TERMINAL, ...   76
    in Cannon Field, Hampton Hill, Middlesex,
    of the Hounslow Heath Base, measured by
    General William Roy in 1784, as restored to
    commemorate the 200th anniversary of his birth,
    4 May, 1726. From a photograph taken in 1927.

CHAPTER I

The Elizabethan Surveyors, their Work, and its Influence on the British Cartography of the Seventeenth Century

I

CHRISTOPHER SAXTON, PHILIP LEA, AND THE QUARTERMASTER'S MAP

IN this chapter it is proposed to deal with the beginnings of the systematic construction of maps in this country, as illustrated by our English cartographers of the time of Queen Elizabeth, and distinguished by the surveys of Christopher Saxton, a Yorkshire man, and of John Norden, a native of Somerset.

We know little, and, indeed, there seems little to learn of the work and method of the Elizabethan surveyors in detail. We can, at most, only judge of them by the results they achieved.

Of the two men mentioned as pioneers in this matter, Christopher Saxton, of Dunningley, a hamlet of the parish of West Ardsley or Woodchurch, between Leeds and Wakefield, in Yorkshire, was born in either 1542 or 1544, according to two discordant statements he makes in depositions now in the Public Record Office—qualified, both of them, however, by the phrase "or thereabouts". Having regard to the dates of the months of these depositions, the difference between them is really one of about two years and five months.

He was alive in 1608, and, probably, two years later, but the actual date of his death remains unascertainable.

Saxton has been described as "servant to Thomas Seckford", who was Master of the Requests to Queen Elizabeth, and was, therefore, an influential court official, and, if we are to judge from his benefactions to his native town of Woodbridge, in Suffolk, a wealthy and important personage. The survey of England and Wales is attributable to the influence and support and the financial assistance of Seckford and, no doubt, of his friends. There is graphic testimony to the interest of Seckford in Saxton's work in the fact that his coat of arms is uniformly engraved on Saxton's maps.

A contemporary writer, William Harrison, in his "Description of Britaine", in the first edition of Holinshed's *Chronicles* (1577), refers no doubt to Saxton and Seckford in the following paragraph, which, it will be observed, was printed when Saxton's survey of England and Wales was approaching completion. (After setting out an incomplete list and particulars of the counties, the author continues):

And these I had of a friende of myne, by whose traveyle and hys maisters excessive charges I doubt not, but my country men eare long shall see all Englande set foorth in severall shyres after the maner that Ortelius hath dealt wyth other countries of the mayne, to the great benefite of our nation and everlasting fame of the aforesayde parties.

The following recital from the licence dated July 22nd, 1577, to print and publish his maps for a period of ten years, is even more explicit:

Whereas Christopher Saxton servaunte to oure trustie and welbeloved Thomas Sekeford Esquier Master of Requestes unto us hathe already (at the greate coste expenses and charges of his said master) traveyled throughe the greatest parte of this oure Realme of Englande and hathe to the greate pleasure and commoditie of us and our lovinge subjectes uppon the perfecte viewe of a greate nomber of the severall Counties and Sheires of oure said Realme drawen oute and sett fourthe diverse trewe and pleasaunte mappes chartes or platts of the same counties together withe the Cities Townes Villages and Ryvers therein conteyned vearie diligentlye and exactly donne and extendithe [intendith] yf God graunte hym lief further to travell therein to cause the same platts and discriptions to be well and fayre Ingraven in plates of copper and to be after Impressed and stamped out of the same as well to the commoditie of oure subjectes as to all other that shall have pleasure to see and peruse the same. . . .

It may be noted that there is no trace of any direct allocation of public funds in support of Saxton's labours. He had, however, certain grants from the Crown of manors and offices of trust, in the years 1574 (Grant of Grigston Manor, etc., in Suffolk); 1575 (Grant of the reversion to the Receivership of the Hospital of St John of Jerusalem in England); 1580 (Grant of land in the parish of St Sepulchre without Newgate, for 60 years, at a rental of 3s. 4d., with permission to build one or more houses).

Saxton was also gratified with a grant of Armorial Bearings in 1579—the year in which his atlas of County Maps appeared. The grant was not then, it seems, recorded at the College of Arms, but is known from a transcript of the warrant and a sketch of the arms in the Wood MSS. in the Bodleian Library. The then Norroy, King of Arms for the Northern Province, was, in 1927, good enough to have these arms re-drawn, certified and recorded.

This outline is all that can be usefully offered of the personal foundation of Saxton's great work, though a certain amount of collateral family history can be extracted from wills in the Registry at York, and an account of Saxton's family from materials accumulated here and elsewhere has been recently published in the *Miscellanea* of the Thoresby Society, where it may be consulted.

As to the method and technical basis of the survey nothing is apparently known. The system of surveying of the early cartographers merits investigation, but the materials for such a study are not abundant. Something can be gathered from sketches of surveyors, and their instruments, and even from diagrams and calculations found here and there in the foregrounds and ornamental margins of plans and views of towns of the sixteenth and seventeenth centuries and in the margins of maps of the same period; and it is to be noted that Leonard Digges had, as early as the middle of the sixteenth century, apparently, described and figured a *Theodolite*, and that "The Boke of Measuryng of Lande" by Sir Richarde de Benese had been printed about 1537. The recent researches of Miss E. G. R. Taylor, published in the *Geographical Journal*, have also thrown light on this subject, and the figure here reproduced of Waldseemüller's Polymetrum, from Reisch's *Margarita Philosophica Nova*, of 1512, showing a combination of the theodolite and the plane-table, as now known to us, is of very great interest in this connection.

It is obvious that, in default of instruments of precision, some sort of triangulation of an elementary and imperfect character must have been resorted to. Triangulation is, of course, an essential feature in accurate mapping.

The only indication we have in connection with Saxton's perambulations is contained in a letter issued to authorize his proceedings in the Principality of Wales in 1576, in which occur the following instructions:

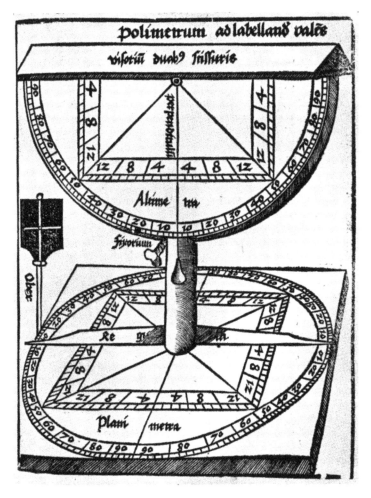

Waldseemüller's Polymetrum.
From Reisch's *Margarita Philosophica Nova*, 1512.

To all Justices of peace mayo^rs and oth^rs etc w^tin the severall Shieres of Wales that whereas the bearer hereof Christopher Saxton is appointed by her Matie under her signe and signet to set forth and describe in cartes particularlie all the shieres in Wales that the said Justices shal be aiding and assisting unto him to see him conducted unto any towre castle highe place or hill to view that countrey and that he may be accompanied wth ij or iij honest men such as do best know the cuntrey for the better accomplishement of that service and that at his departure from any towne or place that he hath taken the view of the said towne do set forth a horseman that can speke both Welshe and Englishe to safe conduct him to the next market Towne, etc.

The success of Saxton's survey was equal to its novelty, and it at once took an important place in the world's cartography. In a period which is said to have been one of nine years (though no specific authority exists, apparently, for this limitation) Saxton surveyed and mapped the whole of England and Wales, and, by 1579, he had compiled and published his series of 34 maps of the counties, some of them individually and others grouped together, with a frontispiece general map of the whole area. Individual maps are dated in the successive years of their original appearance, the two earliest being of 1574 (Oxfordshire, Bucks and Berks in one sheet, and Norfolk).

A little later, probably about 1584, he published a large general map of England and Wales, in 20 sheets, measuring as a whole, about $5\frac{1}{2}$ feet wide by $4\frac{1}{2}$ feet high, on a scale which appears to be one of between $7\frac{1}{2}$ and 8 miles to the inch.

It is only quite recently that this map has been recognized by cartographers. No copy of the original is known to have survived, but its existence can be deduced from copies printed from the original plates very much cut about and altered in all the marginal details, and with the roads added, by Philip Lea, a hundred years later, in 1687. By a piece of extraordinary good luck there have been preserved in the British Museum impressions taken from these plates by Lea, as trial prints in the course of his manipulations of the originals. These impressions show two large blanks, namely the whole of the right-hand top corner, filled originally by Saxton's decorative title, and the panels on the left side of the map. In this state the arms of Seckford appear towards the right-hand bottom corner; the particulars relating to the initial meridian adopted (the island of St Mary in the Azores) in the left-hand bottom corner are preserved, and the sea is decorated with a large number of ships of the end of the sixteenth century.

Lea engraved his own title in the place of that of Saxton, of which latter some traces remain, however, distinguishable on the plate; he replaced the Seckford arms with those of Peter Mews, Bishop of Winchester; he restored the panels on the left of the map, but he erased the Isle of Man, and re-engraved it in a new form; he similarly erased all the large Elizabethan ships, and re-engraved in their places, in most cases, ships of the period of James II, and he inserted roads throughout the map and touched up the details in other particulars. This transformation, and the attempt to work back from it to the original in every detail present for the student a cartographical puzzle of great interest.

Lea's map was, it would seem, frequently reprinted. A copy which is known bears the imprint, in place of that of Lea, of John Bowles & Son, which carries us on to the middle of the eighteenth century, and it seems to have been frequently advertised by the Bowles family, and, finally, by Robert Sayer as late as 1763. Thus the plates of Saxton's large map were in use for something more than a century and a half, and it does not appear certain that they were effectively displaced until the appearance of John Cary's "New Map of England and Wales with Part of Scotland" in eighty-one sheets, and on a scale of 5 miles to the inch, in 1794.

The map known as the "Quartermaster's Map" is, it appears, what may be called a "derivative" from that of Saxton. It was engraved by Hollar, for the publisher Thomas Jenner, in 1644, for the use of the armies then in the field in the contest between the Parliament and the Crown, and, upon examination, it is clear that it was closely copied from Saxton's original—the only source in fact for such a map then available. In particular it gives the original Saxton design of the Isle of Man, and has, of course, no roads. Of this map Jenner issued another edition, dated 1671, on which some of the principal roads were inserted. John Garrett took over the plates from Jenner and issued an undated impression with an amended title and large additions to the roads, in 1688, and, in the next century, the plates had come into the possession of John Rocque, who printed from them, without alteration, in 1752. There is even an impression known which was published on paper water-marked "1799", thus carrying on the design and outline of Saxton's map of England and Wales for more than two centuries. Hollar, to make the map compact, so that it might be folded into a small compass for the pocket, limited the surface engraved to that of the land, and reduced the sheets to the number of six.

An observation seems necessary here on the question

whether Saxton's general map of England and Wales is to be regarded as an entirely original work, or whether he may not have drawn to some extent on earlier sources.

There is, in fact, only one map of any size which might have been of assistance, namely, the map of the British Isles completed at Duisburg by the celebrated Mercator in 1564, and thus twenty years earlier than the suggested date (1584) of Saxton's map of England and Wales.

Of the former map copies in the engraved state have recently been found in Italy, and the books of the famous printing establishment at Antwerp of Christopher Plantin contain records showing that copies were, in the ordinary course of business, sent over to England.

Thus, while no copy is now known in this country, Saxton most probably had the map in his possession at the time of his surveys and their publication.

Nevertheless, an inspection and comparison of the two maps do not suggest to the eye any concordance of form or outline, and we are, therefore, justified in assuming that Saxton's map was an entirely new one, and founded exclusively on his own original surveys.

To revert to the county maps of Saxton. They are not discussed individually, as copies are available for study in all the principal libraries and they are dealt with in detail in standard works. Attention should, however, be called to the re-issue of the atlas in 1645, from the original plates, by Web, which, in general, are only altered by being re-dated; to further doubtful reprints of these maps, in whole, or in part, by Peter Stent; to their use (some of them only, however, and these very much altered in their marginal details and to some extent on the map surface) by Philip

Lea in 1699, with a new title, and to a final re-issue of some of this material by Wildey about 1720.

Passing from Saxton's great national work, it is necessary to mention his private work as a surveyor in the later days of his life. The completion of his map of England and Wales, and probably also the death of his patron Seckford a little later (in January 1587–8), must have left Saxton without public employment or patronage, and thereafter he is only known by a series of private surveys and maps, which have a range in time from 1596 to 1606.

They are of interest, but of no real cartographical importance. The most important of them, perhaps, made in 1596 for the celebrated Dr Dee, at that time newly appointed Warden of Manchester College, was a map of Manchester itself which, unfortunately, has been lost or destroyed; another of Dewsbury, made in 1600, is now in the Dewsbury Free Library.

II

JOHN NORDEN, PHILIP SYMONSON, AND ESTATE SURVEYS

THE life and work of Saxton's contemporary, John Norden, are of considerable interest. Born in Somerset, according to his own statement, we do not know more of his place of birth. The year was 1548, and he died either in 1625 or 1626. He was employed as surveyor to the Crown and to the Duchy of Cornwall, and the main part of his cartographical work may be classed under the heading: "Estate Surveys".

Norden did undertake, however, a general survey and description of the counties of England and Wales, but for the want of adequate financial and official support, of which he bitterly complains, this venture was not a success. He succeeded in publishing (in 1593) "An historicall & chorographicall Description of Middlesex", and (in 1598) "The Description of Hartfordshire", both with maps on a small scale, but distinguished by a delineation of the principal roads. Other counties were surveyed, but Norden's descriptions and maps were not in these cases published by him, though some of the maps appeared in his lifetime. The following were, it seems, engraved and published independently: Essex (1594), published with the full text of the description of this county, by Sir Henry Ellis in 1840; Surrey, engraved by Charles Whitwell, in 1594; Sussex in 1595, and Hampshire without date, but not later than the end of the reign of Elizabeth (1603). A description of Northamptonshire, but without any map, dated 1590, was printed in 1720, and one of Cornwall, accompanied by maps of the hundreds and several small views, in 1728. In connection with his project for a general survey, Norden printed also (1596) a "Preparative to his *Speculum Britanniae*". His "Surveyors Dialogue" appeared in 1607, with reprints in 1610 and 1618. Two modern reprints of this work are also known, dated 1758 and 1855 respectively.

In the folio edition of Camden's *Britannia*, the last Latin edition, published in 1607, and of which an English version, the translation by Philemon Holland, appeared in two editions (1610 and 1637), the maps of Hampshire, Kent, Surrey and Sussex, besides those of Hertfordshire and Middlesex, are stated to be from Norden's surveys, while forty of the maps of this series are founded on those of Saxton.

Norden invented the triangular tables of distances, which he published in his "England, An Intended Guyde for English Travailers, Shewing in generall, how far one Citie, and many Shire-Townes in England, are distant from other. Together with the Shires in particular: and the chiefe townes in every of them. With a generall Table, of the most of the principall Townes in Wales. Invented and collected by John Norden", London, 1625. This very clever arrangement was republished in other guides for travellers during the seventeenth century, and has been made use of in a variety of cartographical publications and guides from their first appearance until our own time, and should be a standing monument of the author, though it is not the fact that Norden has, in modern times at least, been credited with this invention.

Although it has been for a long time a matter of doubt whether or no Norden the surveyor was identical with John Norden the writer of a series of books of a devotional character and of certain poems, which appeared in this name, this doubt has recently been removed and the identity is now finally established. The earliest known, "A Pensive Man's Practise. Newly Corrected and Enlarged", is of 1585, and of this many subsequent editions appeared. Twenty titles of works of this character are to be credited to Norden. The last: "Pathway to Patience in all Manner of Afflictions", which was published in 1626, and perhaps after his death, is a pathetic contribution to his personal history, for it is associated with the neglect, starvation and obscurity in which he ended his days.

In the introduction to Sir Henry Ellis's publication of Norden's description of Essex, issued by the Camden Society in 1840, a good deal of interesting information is given as to Norden's official position and employment, and as to his salary and other forms of remuneration, original documents being set out. He was for many years in the regular service of the Crown and of the Duchy of Cornwall, and his son, also John, was associated with him in his surveys.

While his few printed maps are only important from the fact that they are the first published in England upon which the roads are drawn, Norden's work as a surveyor is much more extensive than that of Saxton. His survey of the "Honor of Windsor" for James I, dated 1607, showing the castle and its precincts, and the town of Windsor, with all the several parks and chases belonging to the royal estate, is a work of considerable interest and beauty, and is valuable as characteristic of estate mapping at the beginning of the seventeenth century in its best and most artistic development. The maps, or plans, are seventeen in number, measuring each about 424 mm. in height by 570 mm. in width, but with some variations in size. They are drawn in water-colour on vellum sheets with suitable decorative effects. The titles and dedications are ornamental works of the illuminator's art, and tables of the red and fallow deer in the various parks are annexed. Two copies were made, and have been, happily, preserved, though both of them were at one time in private hands. The King's copy is in the British Museum (Harleian MS.), and the copy made for Henry, Prince of Wales, has recently reached a secure resting-place in the library of Windsor Castle.

Another, and an even more important work of private survey, is that of the estates of Sir Michael Stanhope on the coast of Suffolk, in the neighbourhood of Orford. Here an area of 15,000 acres was mapped, including a long coast-line. The coast was, it seems, very carefully surveyed, in order to show and account for a large area of "Beach", part of the manorial property, and this delineation of the coast-line is of great geographical value in the study of the changes in the shore by both erosion and accretion which have taken place during the past three centuries, interesting both to the geographer and the geologist. Sir Michael Stanhope's Estate, surveyed in 1600 and 1601, was drawn on twenty-eight sheets, in the same style and manner as those of the Windsor survey. The estate having been divided, the plans have been divided also between the present land-owners, a portion (sheets I to X) being now in a solicitor's office in Woodbridge, and the remainder (sheets XI to XXVIII except sheet XIII, which has been lost) being in the estate office at Chillesford Lodge, near Orford. Tables of the acreages, with distinction of woodland, arable, etc., set out in detail, and showing portions on lease, in hand, and so on, are annexed to these maps, and are themselves of historical importance. These are the most important examples of John Norden's cartographical work as an estate surveyor of which notice should be taken. In much of this work his son, of the same name, was associated with him.

A considerable work of survey and inquiry undertaken by the two Nordens, with other assistance, was that of the manors and estates of the Duchy of Cornwall in the counties of Cornwall and Somerset (made in 1609–1616), which, however, did not take a cartographical form, and does not, therefore, specially concern us here. The results of this extensive work are now in the Royal Library in two quarto volumes, as originally presented to Sir Francis Bacon, then President of the Council of the Duchy.

Some other work of a similar character can be assigned to Norden, but none of it is of particular importance, and his reputation as a working surveyor and constructor of maps and plans may well rest on the two magnificent productions to which I have referred.

This review of the work of our two great Elizabethan surveyors and cartographers would be incomplete without some mention of a contemporary, Philip Symonson, who is particularly known by his large map of the county of Kent which illustrates Lambarde's second edition of his "Perambulation of Kent", and appears to have been published in 1596, although there is ground for suspecting an original impression of an earlier date. Symonson was surveyor to the corporation which managed the bridge estates and maintained the great bridge at Rochester over the Medway on the London-Dover road, and in that capacity he surveyed and mapped the estates of the corporation. He died in 1598.

There were other estate maps drawn in the same manner at this period. It seems that some of them survive in the bursaries of colleges in the Universities of Oxford and Cambridge, and possibly in some other public and estate and private offices. For instance, a beautiful example, showing the college property in the parish of Gamlingay, in Cambridgeshire, a map dated 1601, the work of a surveyor named Thomas Langdon, exists in the bursary of Merton College, Oxford.

There are thus brought together the facts in an illustrative, but not in an entirely exhaustive form, of course, of the beginnings in England of a national cartography, and from them can be deduced the influence of these foundations on the production of maps during the century following, until, in the last quarter of that century, Ogilby, Seller, Morgan, Senex, Morden and Moll built up a new school, based upon advances in cartographical and geographical knowledge, but showing, on the whole, little advance in the art of map delineation.

III

THE COUNTY MAPS OF ENGLAND AND WALES OF THE SEVENTEENTH CENTURY

Two important series of county maps of the beginning of the seventeenth century must be classed with the cartographical work of Saxton and Norden. The earliest is the set of maps illustrating the folio Latin edition of Camden's *Britannia* published in 1607, and already referred to. These maps are reductions to the size of the double page of the folio volumes in which they occur. They were engraved, some by William Hole, and some by William Kip. Besides the six attributed to John Norden and the forty bearing the name of Christopher Saxton, one (Pembrokeshire) is the work of a Welsh draughtsman, and six (Cornwall, Dorset, Wilts, Essex, Rutland and Staffordshire) bear no indication of original authorship, and may have been taken from a combination of the original designs of Saxton and Norden. It is to be observed that in the use of Norden's designs in 1607 the roads are uniformly omitted, and roads do not appear upon any map of the series.

It is not improbable that the small map of Kent entitled a "Carde of this Shyre", which appears to be the map mentioned in an original manuscript of Lambarde's "Perambulation of Kent" dated as early as 1570, may have supplied a foundation for the map in the *Britannia*. The authorship of this map is unknown, but, if one is to judge by the appearance of the design in its details and the ornamentation, it may be said to be highly probable that it was drawn by Saxton, whose map of Middlesex, Surrey, Sussex and Kent appeared in 1575. When we compare the 1607 version of Norden's map of Kent with the "Carde", discrepancies of style, outline and detail are obvious throughout, and no one would assume, on an inspection, that the two maps had anything in the nature of a common origin. There are three versions of this "Carde", distinguishable by alterations made on the plate and particularly by the insertion of roads on the later copies.

John Speed, who must have drawn, but without acknowledgment, upon both Saxton and Norden, began the publication of his individual maps of the counties of England and Wales in 1605; many of them are dated 1610, and the complete collection appeared in 1611, with the title "The Theatre of the Empire of Great Britaine". There were a number of reprints up to 1676, and, thereafter, the plates were used, very much worn down, for the publication of the maps in atlas form in at least four issues (1713, 1736 (?), 1743 and 1777 *circa*).

To complete one's knowledge of the cartographical development which, throughout the seventeenth and even well into the eighteenth century, followed Saxton and Norden and their work as its foundation, notice must be taken of a

Northamptonshire and other Midland Counties of England. Engraved by Peter Keer, 1599.

After Christopher Saxton's Map of 1576.

series of reductions, or epitomes, of the county maps of Saxton. They commence with a set of such maps engraved by Peter Keer in 1599 (those few which are dated bearing this year), but of which no impressions are known earlier than 1617, when these maps were used to illustrate an epitome of Camden's *Britannia* published at Amsterdam. The same plates were re-used with the titles of the maps in English, in place of the original Latin, in a little oblong book entitled: "England, Wales, Scotland and Ireland Described and abridged with yᵉ Historie Relation of things worthy memory from a farr larger Voulume Done by John Speed", of which the first issue is believed to be of 1620. Other editions exist of 1627, 1662, 1666 and 1676. John Bill also, in 1626, published an abridgment of Camden's *Britannia*, illustrated by county maps similar to those of Keer.

IV

THE ART AND TECHNIQUE AND GENERAL HISTORY OF THE CARTOGRAPHY OF THE SIXTEENTH AND SEVENTEENTH CENTURIES

IT remains to examine the art and technique of the early period, and to institute a slight comparison with contemporaneous progress on the continent of Europe.

By Saxton's time, the practice of orienting maps with the north at the top had become well settled, and the question of orientation does not arise.

That of the initial meridian was quite unsolved, and there

was no agreement on the subject amongst cartographers. Some point in the Azores, or the Canaries, was most favoured at this time, but it was not till 1634 that the French Government of Richelieu and Louis XIII fixed upon Ferro (Île de Fer), the most westerly of the Canaries, as the basis upon which French maps were to be drawn. This initial meridian was maintained on French maps up to the Revolution of 1789.

As has already been noted, Saxton founded on the island of St Mary, the most easterly of the group of the Azores. In England a vague westerly initial meridian remained in use until 1676, apparently, when London was adopted by John Seller in his map of Herts. Later, St Paul's Cathedral and, finally, Greenwich, now stereotyped for all time by the world-map on the scale of one-millionth, were adopted.

If it is desired to pursue this technical subject, as one of historical or scientific interest, a considerable mass of material can easily be discovered. Perhaps the most useful discussion of this subject in its earlier aspects is to be found in Herman Moll's *Atlas Manuale*, published in 1709.

Of scale there is much variety, naturally, in early maps, and even until quite modern days, and it will not be practicable to attempt to deal with this point historically here.

When one comes to look critically at the design and detail of early maps, one is struck with the small amount of pictorial information displayed on the surface delineated, as compared with the maps overloaded with details to which the modern map-maker has accustomed us. The outline of land and water, including in the latter the sea-shore lines, the extent of inland lakes and the line of the principal rivers, the situation of the principal agglomerations of human settlement, some feeble effort to represent high lands, hills and mountains, and perhaps forest areas, is all that strikes the eye. It is in fact all that the early cartographers could deal with, from a want both of knowledge of geographical details and of the acquired art of technical representation of variety of surface conditions.

There were no roads, and the first attempt to offer facilities for travel and movement was that of marking bridges where they existed over important rivers. This is seen on Saxton's maps. It will be remembered that one of the three obligations imposed on all the land of England from Saxon times (*trinoda necessitas*) was that of the repair of bridges (maintenance of communications); the two others being the maintenance of the castles, or garrisons (public order), and service for defence of the realm. Norden and Symonson introduced roads, but it was not until after the official measurement of the roads of England and Wales by John Ogilby, and the publication of his road-maps in 1675, that roads became a regular feature of all maps of any size, such as those of Seller and Morgan (from 1676 onwards).

The publication of the results of Ogilby's road-survey was, however, slightly anticipated by the appearance, as I have already noted, of some of the principal lines of roads on the "Quartermaster's Map" of 1671. One notices particularly on our sixteenth century county maps the care which was taken to insert parks as a special feature, the privilege of enclosure for maintaining deer and other wild animals for the chase being by prescription, or royal grant, and thus of importance. As regards hills and high ground, both Saxton and Norden adopt a shading to give relief to these features based upon the idea of light falling from the west, and trees are shaded upon the same conventional principle. A form of horizontal shading was used by Saxton to denote the sea-bordèr along the coast-line, which is still amongst the technical features of expression used in the construction of maps.

In examining scientific and literary progress in Europe in the sixteenth century, as indeed in earlier periods, it must be borne in mind how small at that period was the world of learning. In this limited sphere of common interest and common knowledge, any development, any definite progress, soon became universal. Thus, in studying the growth of English cartography, we must, to obtain an intelligent appreciation of the situation from time to time, at least glance at the state of matters in the narrow field of central Europe.

In the fifteenth century the collections of maps drawn on the data supplied by what then remained of Ptolemy's *Geographia* began to be regarded, no doubt, as obsolete, while the portolan charts of the coast-lines of the Mediterranean and of the Atlantic coasts of Europe and Africa, being entirely in manuscript, had only a small publicity.

But, the discoveries of the great adventurers were bearing fruit; the demand for a cartographical basis for further progress had become insistent, and at the same time the arts of printing and of engraving on wood and copper were being developed.

In these circumstances, the grouping together of maps in the form of what we now know as an atlas (following the title adopted by Mercator for such a series) became of evident utility. In 1570 then, Abraham Ortelius put together a collection of maps, to which he gave the title

Theatrum Orbis Terrarum, a volume re-issued with additional maps, through a considerable series of years.

The atlas of Gerhard Mercator, held back, it is said, to give his friend Ortelius priority of sale, did not appear until after the death of the former, in 1594, and, from the end of the century until the middle of the century following, the Dutch and Flemish school held the field in the production of large and splendid atlases, running, some of them, to eleven or twelve ponderous volumes. Moses Pitt, at Oxford, drew upon the same Dutch material in his "English Atlas" of 1680.

In France it was not until 1594 that anything in the nature of a national atlas was attempted. A year or two earlier Maurice Bouguereau, a publisher of Tours, engaged Gabriel Tavernier, of the Antwerp family of cartographers, to engrave maps of certain of the French provinces, which he published in that year under the title *Le Théâtre François*. The maps so produced were re-published with the addition of others from time to time. These publications have little of individual character, or style, being based almost exclusively on Dutch originals, but they had priority in point of time in France over the original cartographical work—much better known to fame—of Nicolas Sanson and his successors, to which the second chapter now following is devoted.

CHAPTER II

The French School of Cartography of the Seventeenth Century

I

NICOLAS SANSON AND HIS ENGRAVERS AND PUBLISHERS

THE cartographical activity in France in the half-century covering the period 1594 to 1644, and thus partially parallel in time with the development of cartography in England dealt with in the first chapter, being represented by Maurice Bouguereau, of Tours, and the engraver he employed, Gabriel Tavernier, Jean Le Clerc and his widow and successor, Melchior Tavernier, Pierre Mariette, Nicolas Tassin, Nicolas Berey, and Jean Boisseau, is itself preceded by the isolated effort of Guillaume Postel (a map of France dated 1570, and dedicated to Charles IX), and is associated with that of François de La Guillotière (a map of France in nine sheets, engraved on wood, and presented to Louis XIII in 1612, or 1613; its production having involved the author in a labour of sixteen years, 1596–1612).

This preliminary period of progress in the art of map-construction in France, while it precedes the development of the specially French School of Cartography of the seventeenth century with which the name of Nicolas Sanson, as its founder, is particularly associated, does not connect itself with that development as being in any way a basis, or foundation for the work of Sanson, who, perhaps, sought inspiration directly in the work of the Dutch and Flemish cartographical school, which had achieved an enormous output in the early part of the seventeenth century, rather than in any previous publications of his own country. It is indeed a subject of remark that Sanson, and the engravers he employed, as well as the Tavernier family, were all except one, either Flemings or of the border province of Picardy.

Whatever may be its genesis and early associations, the School of French Cartography of which Nicolas Sanson and his sons, the Jaillot family, and the two Robert de Vaugondys are typical exponents, is a productive unit, if its characteristics may be so expressed, and it is, therefore, selected for special consideration in connection with the advance it marks in map production.

Nicolas Sanson was born in 1600, at Abbeville, in Picardy, and he died in 1667, in Paris. He came of an old Picardy family of Scottish descent. His first publication is said to have been a map of ancient Gaul, in six sheets, which he had completed when he was only eighteen years old, but which was not printed until 1629. According to Robert de Vaugondy he was obliged to establish himself in Paris in consequence of difficulties with his publisher, Melchior Tavernier. His three sons, Nicolas, Adrien and Guillaume, assisted him, and the two last-named succeeded him in his geographical work; the eldest, Nicolas, having been killed in the day of the *Barricades*, in Paris, in 1648. Adrien died in 1708, and Guillaume in 1703. It was to these latter that the first Jaillot (Alexis Hubert) owed the materials upon which was constructed his great atlas.

The earliest complete collection of Sanson's maps, made up with both a printed title-page and a printed list of

Section from Nicolas Sanson's map, engraved by R. Cordier, 1654, of the *Anciens Royaumes de Mercie et East-Angles*. From the atlas, the *Cartes Générales de Toutes les Parties du Monde*. 1658.

contents, is of the year 1658. The list contains 113 titles. This is a general atlas, and was published by Sanson in Paris. The title runs:

> *Cartes Générales de Toutes les Parties du Monde, ou les Empires, Monarchies, Republiques, Estats, Peuples, etc. de l'Asie, de l'Africque, de l'Europe, et de l'Americque, tant Anciens que Nouveaux, sont exactement remarqués, et distingués suivant leur estendue. Par le Sieur Sanson d'Abbeville, Géographe ordinaire du Roy. A Paris, Chez l'Autheur, Dans le Cloistre de Sainct Germain l'Auxerrois, pres et joignant la grande Porte du Cloistre, et Chez Pierre Mariette, rue Sainct Jacques, a l'Espérance. MDCLVIII. Avec Privilege du Roy pour vingt ans.*

Another atlas, with the same title, is in the British Museum, dated 1667, and, being published after the death of Sanson, by his two surviving sons, is: *Par les Sieurs Sanson d'Abeville, Geographes ordinaires du Roy.* A copy of the atlas of 1658, in the Bibliothèque Nationale, in Paris, contains 124 maps. But a recent examination of this and the other Sanson atlases in Paris shows that they are very unsatisfactory examples, and are of little assistance in settling the cartobibliography of the Sansons.

Of the dated maps in an atlas without title, or list, in my collection, which contains 100 maps, the dates are as follows: 1632, 1; 1640, 2; 1641, 2; 1642, 3; 1643, 2; 1644, 1; 1646, 2; 1647, 1; 1648, 11; 1650, 8; 1651, 5; 1652, 8; 1653, 6; 1654, 10. Thirty-eight of the plates are, however, undated, and the dates which exist are not with certainty the original dates of impression, and some of the engravings are, possibly, not the work of Sanson at all. With these qualifications, the enumeration above may be accepted as giving some indication of Sanson's progressive activity in the production of maps during his career as a cartographer. An analysis of the names of publishers and engravers found on these maps shows that Sanson's associates in their production were, from an early date, Melchior Tavernier and Pierre Mariette, both as publishers and engravers, and, as principal engravers simply, A. Peyrounin, R. Cordier, of Abbeville, and Jean Sommer, or Somer, who calls himself *Pruthenus*, or the Prussian. Of these three engravers, Cordier is much the most skilful, and his work merits careful study, as a development of the graphic art as applied to the production of maps in a very delicate form.

The first of the above series of maps is of rather special interest, as being the earliest map known of the postal roads of France (1632). It was followed (in 1634) by one of the rivers, the water-highways of France. These both bear notes touching their origin which are of a certain historical interest.

The *Carte Geographicque des Postes qui traversent la France* was published by Tavernier, who thus addresses the reader:

Au Lecteur. L'Estat de toutes les Postes qui traversent la France m'etant tombé depuis peu entre les mains je priay le Sr. N. Sanson d'Abbeville de me le dresser en vne Carte Geographicque quil ma aussy tost rendu telle que je la p̃te sil sy trouve a augmenter ou diminuer men advertissant je le feray pour le contenter et servir le publicq. a Dieu.

The other early map, that of the rivers of France, was issued by Pierre Mariette. Its title is: *Carte des Rivieres de la France curieusement recherchée Par Nicolas Sanson Ing^er, et Geog^r ord^re du Roy.* In an address, also to the reader, engraved on the map, speaking of the rivers, the author says:

J'espere Amy lecteur que tu en trouveras un grand nombre qui ne se sont veus ny dans les Cartes Generales, ny mesme dans les plus Particulieres. Encor en ferai-je voir d'advãtage quand je doñeray au jour les Cartes de toute la France, a quoy le Sieur Tavernier nespargne point la despense, ny moy ma peine pour les mettre tout en estat quelles puissent servir comodement au publicq : tu nous advertiras sy tu as quelque chose quy nous y puisse ayder et ce. pendant tu auras le Contentement de ce petit dessein des Rivieres de la France. Adieu.

While the map of the post roads was enlarged and much embellished later in the *Atlas Nouveau*, the promise of an improved map of the rivers seems never to have been realized.

There exists in manuscript, in the library of the Ministry of War, in Paris, a very large map, showing both the roads and rivers, without date and bearing no evidence of origin. There is no reason, however, for associating this map with the Sansons or their successors. It was drawn up on the indications supplied by the Intendants of the several généralités, and measures 8 feet $4\frac{1}{2}$ inches in width by 7 feet 3 inches in height, and is in bright colours.

It is proper to notice, as a part of the cartographic output of the Sansons, the small, quarto atlases, issued separately for Europe, Asia, Africa and America, with interleaved descriptive text. The first volume which appeared was that for Europe, in 1648. Asia followed in 1652, and Africa and America in 1656. Of each there were several successive issues. In all, Sanson published, it is thought, more than three hundred maps. An attempt has been made to check this figure by collating the maps in all the atlases to be found in the public libraries, but without arriving at any exact conclusion, many of the atlases accessible being more or less made up with extraneous maps and with others which can only doubtfully be attributed to Sanson.

ALEXIUS HUBERTUS IAILLOT, Regis Chriſtianiſſimi Geographus Ordinarius. 1698

Portrait of Alexis Hubert Jaillot, *géographe du roi* (1632–1712).
From the *Atlas Nouveau*, 1698.

II

THE YOUNGER SANSONS AND THE JAILLOT FAMILY OF CARTOGRAPHERS

THE two younger sons of Nicolas Sanson carried on his work and they, in association with the first of the Jaillot family of geographers, Alexis Hubert, no doubt accumulated additional cartographical material; the very large folio atlases published in a number of successive issues towards the end of the seventeenth and at the commencement of the eighteenth century being founded on Sanson's original maps supported by such accumulations. These large atlases began to appear about 1689, preceded by individual maps. They bore the title of the *Atlas Nouveau*.

In the meantime it is desirable to draw attention to the small atlases of Nicolas Tassin published as early as 1640 by Nicolas Berey, whose shop was "*au bout du pont neuf proche les Augustins aux deux globes*", and to whose business the first of the Jaillots (who, in 1664, married the daughter of the house—Jeanne) ultimately succeeded, quite in the orthodox fashion of the faithful apprentice of the moral tales of a century, or more, ago.

This Alexis Hubert Jaillot was born about 1632 in the little hamlet of Avignon, near Saint Claude, in the then Franche-Comté (now in the department of the Jura). He and his brother Simon, both of them sculptors, established themselves in Paris in 1657. Simon does not specially concern us. He is celebrated as the carver of several remarkable figures of Christ in ivory, and, apparently, for his quarrelsome disposition which got him into serious trouble.

He died in 1681. Alexis Hubert, while continuing to work in his original profession, seems to have associated himself with the business of his father-in-law, Nicolas Berey, as a publisher and map producer. The earliest map bearing his name is one dated 1669, two years only after the death of Nicolas Sanson. In 1675 he was appointed "*géographe ordinaire du roy*". It would seem that from this period the scheme of publication of comparatively large atlases, based on the map materials of the elder Sanson and his sons, took form in the hands of Jaillot, and the individual maps of this magnificent series soon began to appear.

An important study by Guillaume Sanson, the *Introduction à l'Étude de la Géographie*, serving as a kind of preface to the great atlas, was printed in 1681, and the first edition of the atlas itself was presented as the *Atlas Nouveau Contenant Toutes les parties du Monde*, to the Dauphin,[1] to whom it was dedicated, in 1689. In 1691 and 1695 there appeared successive editions, with new and additional maps. The latter issue was ornamented with a portrait of Jaillot, engraved after the original painted by Colin. Jaillot received a grant of arms, bearing on the shield three globes, in 1697, which will be found in the manuscript volumes of the *Armorial Général de France* in the Bibliothèque Nationale in Paris.

To the edition of 1695 there is also added a long dedication to the King (Louis XIV), in which Jaillot states that his work on the building up of this atlas had continued during eighteen years, thus carrying its commencement back to about the year 1677, and this seems to accord with the

---

[1] The Grand Dauphin, only son of Louis XIV and Maria Theresa of Austria, who died in April, 1711.

presentation of a copy of a general map of France to the Dauphin as early as 1679.

He was selected as publisher of another important geographical work: *Le Neptune Français, ou Atlas Nouveau des Cartes Marines*, which appeared in 1693, and brought him into relations with the first of the Cassini family, Giovanni Domenico (Jean Dominique), the astronomer, of the new Royal Observatory of Paris completed in 1670, where Cassini commenced observations in the following year. The latter and his colleagues the astronomer members of the Académie des Sciences, were responsible for the determination of the situation of the principal points on the coast by astronomical observation, and thus established, for the first time, the true dimensions of the kingdom of France, of which the breadth had previously been much exaggerated in accordance with the erroneous figures of the Mediterranean evolved by Ptolemy. Jaillot dying in 1712, was succeeded by one of his sons, who, in his turn, gave place to his grandson, and the establishment continued a centre of cartographical production until at least as late as about 1741, publishing the annual postal guides, to which reference is made later, until the year 1779, always, apparently, in the same house on the Quai des Grands-Augustins in which Nicolas Berey had established himself at least as early as 1640, and which may very possibly be the house now numbered 55 on that quai.

What precedes is in no sense a complete statement of the productivity of the Sanson-Jaillot families. It merely indicates its more salient features. It is also to be observed that, in the middle of the eighteenth century, the Sanson materials were utilized by the two Robert de Vaugondys, father and son, in the construction of atlases, and particularly in the preparation of their great *Atlas Universel*, referred to later.

A very distinct and special publication undertaken by the successive members of the Jaillot family, which may be regarded as of a certain collateral geographical importance, and thus ought not to be passed over here, was that of the official, or rather, perhaps, semi-official handbook to the postal system of France, the *Liste Générale des Postes de France*, which, from 1708 to 1779 appeared annually, and occasionally twice in the year, in the first instance engraved throughout, and towards the end of the series (from 1772) in print. From 1716, a small map of the post-roads of France was issued with this little book, giving it a carto-graphical value and interest. The licences to publish establish the succession in the Jaillot family as publishers as follows: 1708, Alexis Hubert; 1724, Bernard Jean Hyacinthe; 1728 and 1749, Bernard Antoine, and 1756 and 1769, Chauvigné-Jaillot. They were all successively Geographers to the King.

A curiosity, bibliographically, at all events, is the ap-pearance, alongside of the legitimate issues of this guide to the posts, of numerous piracies. They must have been numerous, as they are denounced regularly in the notices inserted in these guides, and in those which succeeded them under other titles until well into the nineteenth century. The *priviléges* throughout contain severe penalties in case of infringement and as late as 1800 one finds their publishers denounced as "*vils contrefacteurs*". As a matter of fact these pirated volumes have only survived in a very few examples, and, up to now, not more than five copies of such publica-tions have been identified.

The Jaillot geographical establishment came to an end in 1780, when it had attained to a continuous existence of more than a century. The last of the family was Jean Baptiste Michel Renou de Chauvigné-Jaillot, who had come into the business as husband, as it appears, of one of the grand-daughters of Alexis Hubert. He died April 5th, 1780, and in the following year the whole of the stock-in-trade was disposed of by public auction.

The *Atlas Nouveau*, in an issue of 1696, edited by Pierre Mortier, at Amsterdam, contains 136 maps, and is in two volumes. It also has, interleaved with the associated maps, twenty-eight sheets of engraved plans and views of the fortresses of Europe, of which there are no less than 196, constituting a series of special interest and beauty, illustrative of the great work of fortification associated with the name of Vauban. These plates were re-used, with additions, making the total of the plans and views up to 275, in a separate publication entitled: *Les Forces de l'Europe, Asie, Afrique et Amérique, ou Description des principales villes, avec leurs fortifications*, by Mortier, at the beginning of the eighteenth century.

The maps designed by Jaillot and his co-workers partook of the errors of the cartography of the sixteenth and seventeenth centuries. The correction of such errors, as they became recognized, would have injured, if not destroyed, the plates as originally engraved, thus involving a great commercial loss; and, consequently, the atlas of Jaillot remained in its original state until it had to give place to the more exact and scientific results achieved by Guillaume Delisle and others of the more technically expert cartographers of the commencement of the eighteenth century, who constructed their maps with a knowledge of the progress made by astronomers in fixing the exact situation of positions on the earth's surface.

It was only in 1696, when it may be said that Jaillot's cartographical work was practically completed, that the first of the Cassinis, in order to bring home to the geographers their errors, and the necessity of co-ordinating their work in the delineation of the earth's surface with the results of astronomical science, drew, on the floor of the eastern saloon of the Observatory of Paris, a planisphere on which were thirty-nine localities, set out according to the then recent calculations.

Several maps of France were published in England by John Senex in the beginning of the eighteenth century on which a coast-outline to show the errors into which Sanson had fallen is engraved, and they are a curious commentary on the defects in the early delineation of the coastal boundaries of the kingdom. The survival of the Jaillot plates, and their continued use, after they had become obsolete geographically, was due, no doubt, in a considerable degree to their beauty of design and decoration, but also, as has already been suggested, to the immense expenditure which would have been involved in substituting for them a new work of equal magnitude.

This is another instance to add to those to which attention has been drawn above in connection with the maps of Saxton and Speed, of what one may call the indecent longevity of maps! It is proper, in dealing with history as illustrated by, or founded on maps, to at all times accept with great reserve and caution undated maps, and those also which bear dates subsequent to those of the original impressions.

It appears that the Amsterdam edition of Jaillot's atlas, by Mortier, of 1696, was a new one, in the sense that the plates were actually re-engraved for that publisher, and it is said that this work is a finer one, from the engraver's point of view, than the original engraved in Paris.

However this may be, from the geographical point of view there is no distinction to be drawn between the two issues of Paris and Amsterdam. A minute comparison of the artistic success of the two ventures does not come within the scope of my present purpose.

III

THE ART OF THE FRENCH SCHOOL OF THE SEVENTEENTH CENTURY AND ITS RELATIONS WITH THE CARTOGRAPHY OF THE FOLLOWING CENTURY

IT is desirable to consider the art developed in the French school, in particular, during the seventeenth century, an art and decoration characteristic of that century, and which came abruptly to an end with the advent of the comparatively exact cartography which immediately followed.

In the early days of engraved maps, their colouring by hand was a regular professional art. It is said of the celebrated Ortelius that he began his life-work in the sixteenth century by collecting and colouring maps for sale at Antwerp, where he was born. In the next century the art of illuminating was much in repute. So much so that we find the cartographer, Jean Boisseau, describing himself, in 1636, as *enlumineur du roi pour les cartes géographiques*, and another map-maker, Nicolas Berey, already referred to as the father-in-law of Alexis Hubert Jaillot, is styled, in 1641, *enlumineur de la reine*. Towards the end of the seventeenth century it was that this art in its application to the maps of Jaillot, attained to its highest point of beauty and elegance. It is true that the engraved plate, with its elaborate decorative panels and other marginal ornamentation, lent itself, at this period, in a special degree, to the judicious addition of water-colour and gilding. The success of this combination is, in fine examples, very striking, and is an interesting, and indeed fascinating, feature of the cartographic success of the artists and colourists employed in the establishments of the Jaillots and Mortier.

Colour on maps is no longer used for decorative purposes, and a distinction must be drawn between such use, and its adaptation to the special geographical features of the map itself. This latter use has, of course, also an early origin. Natural and historical, as well as administrative and local areas were distinguished by the use of colour, and the same may be said, though it was not so settled as a practice, of the distinction of land and water surfaces; but the matter was not carried much further until the latter part of the eighteenth century, in anticipation of the introduction of various methods of printing in colours, from which grew up the extensive use of colour in the essential details of maps; a use which amounts nowadays almost to an abuse, in the hands, at all events, of some of our modern commercial map-makers and publishers.

Of course, maps actually drawn in colours, like the great map of the Austrian Provinces in the Low Countries of the Comte de Ferraris (1770–78), and the immense series of maps of the royal roads in France, made by the engineers and draughtsmen of the government department dealing with these roads (Ponts et Chaussées), present the most complete and natural solution of the use of colour in cartography. To these works of art of a high order reference will be made more fully later.

Associated with design and colouring Jaillot's maps are distinguished by very charming title-panels, or *cartouches*, these being drawn with details to illustrate the natural features, or special produce, or industries which characterize the area represented on the map. They thus present infinite variety, and have even become a subject of collection, to the destruction on a large scale, unfortunately, of the maps themselves. But, without going to this extreme, the study from an art point of view of these designs and of their illumination, in carefully painted specimens, is extremely interesting. It may be noted that the decoration of the sea-surface with ships and marine monsters, and the land-surface with more or less problematical animals, disappears, as a system, during the course of the seventeenth century, and that this ornamentation is altogether wanting on the Sanson-Jaillot series of maps.

It was towards the middle of the eighteenth century that the two Robert de Vaugondys, working, it seems, upon the basis, still preserved, and collected from two different sources into their hands, of the accumulated material of the succession Sanson-Jaillot, produced a very fine, and comparatively modern general atlas, the *Atlas Universel*, which is well-known, and of which copies are still not rare. This atlas, published in 1757, contained 103 maps, but in another issue under the same date, there were added five maps of the post-roads of Europe, that is to say of Italy, Spain, Germany, the British Isles, and France. It is preferable to buy an example with these supplementary maps (making 108 in all), rather than one with the original series alone. The maps of this atlas are also decorated with very well designed and delicately engraved *cartouches*, but it does not appear that they have ever been heightened by the addition of colour or gilding, such decoration having at the date of their appearance long gone out of fashion. An interesting, but altogether incidental feature of this atlas (found in the first issue alone) is the list of original subscribers to whom the 601 large-paper and the 517 small-paper copies were distributed throughout Europe, including the principal booksellers of the more important towns. This list contains a great number of well-known names, and affords a kind of measure of the general interest taken in cartography at this period, which is associated with the appearance (1756) of the earliest sheets of the great Cassini map of France—this year also being that in which the third of the Cassini family (César François) launched his Association for carrying to a completion his magnificent scheme for the preparation of the 173 sheets then proposed constituting the map of France.

The French school founded by the elder Nicolas Sanson may be said to cover roughly a century in time, if we associate with it the *Atlas Universel*, which properly belongs to this school. Its more characteristic period ends, however, with the great atlas of Jaillot, and, if this limitation of time is admitted, it cannot claim much more than a half-century of effective vitality as a school and epoch of map construction, with an influence extending substantially later.

CHAPTER III

Cartography as an Exact Science. Its Development in the Eighteenth Century in France

I

THE CASSINI FAMILY AND THE TRIANGULATION AND MAPPING OF FRANCE

IT is to the eighteenth century that we must attribute the final emergence of cartography as an exact science. That century is distinguished by the first map of any country portraying, as a whole, on a large scale, its surface and superficial characteristics.

The two previous centuries may be regarded as developing tentative stages of progress during which surveyors and cartographers, whose mechanism of work in the field was both imperfect in its practical application, and insufficient, probably, even in theory, were groping for a solution to be supplied by the astronomer on the one hand, and the instrumentally equipped engineer on the other.

The insufficiency of the surveying instruments available in England as late as nearly the end of the century is illustrated by the fact that when, on the invitation of the French Government, it was decided to take the necessary steps on this side of the Channel for connecting, by a triangulation, the observatories of Greenwich and Paris, and General Roy had measured his famous base line on Hounslow Heath, which was completed in 1784, and was the first operation of the kind carried out in this country, he had to wait three full years before the most efficient instrument-maker of the period, Jesse Ramsden, was able to complete a theodolite suitable for his purpose. Thus it was only in 1787 that Roy, having measured in that year a second base in Romney Marsh, was in a position to invite his French colleagues to participate in the connection across the Channel of his triangulation with that of France and with the nearest base in that country laid out along the sea-shore at Dunkirk, measured in the first instance in 1718, and re-measured in 1740.

Ramsden's theodolite is figured in great detail in Roy's communication on his measurement of the Romney Marsh base and the subsequent operations, read before the Royal Society, February 25th, 1790. It still exists, having been presented by George III to the Royal Society, and being now preserved at the Ordnance Survey Office at Southampton. It was in use for 66 years (1787 to 1853).

These operations had the one limited object in view, and are not in themselves the historical foundation of our Ordnance Survey (officially established in 1791 only), the bases for our primary triangulation being now two, one on Salisbury Plain (measured in 1848–9), and the other, for Ireland, at Lough Foyle (measured in 1827–8). It is to be observed, however, that, while these two bases were finally adopted, as many as eight other bases (including those on Hounslow Heath and Romney Marsh) were measured at different times by the ordnance surveyors in various parts of the United Kingdom. This compares with the eighteen bases measured in France for the purpose of the triangulation completed by the Cassinis in 1744, to which reference will presently be made more at length.

From this period of the creation of the British Ordnance Survey at the end of the eighteenth century, which, from a national point of view it is well to bear in mind, it is necessary to go back nearly a century and a half to commence the study of the effort, finally successful, to establish the scientific and exact cartography of the kingdom of France.

The earliest stage of this great undertaking was entirely astronomical, and its starting-point was that of fixing a definite initial meridian, upon the recommendation of a scientific congress assembled by Cardinal Richelieu at Paris in 1630, from which resulted (but four years later) a royal decree (April 25th, 1634) establishing Ferro, the Île de Fer, the most westerly of the group of the Canary Islands, as the locality through which should pass the initial meridian to be adopted by all French navigators, and to be applied in the construction of all French maps from that date forward. On this basis Paris was arbitrarily assumed to be 20° E., and so remained until the Revolution of 1789. The actual difference of longitude between the two points on the earth's surface was actually determined in 1724, when Louis Feuillée, who had been sent out by the French Government, established this difference, between a point on the west coast of Ferro and the Observatory of Paris, as 20° 1′ 45″.

The second stage in the accurate mapping of France has already been alluded to, namely that of the fixing, by astronomical observations, of a sufficient number of points on the coast-lines and superficial extent of the kingdom to establish, once for all, its general topographical distribution as an initial area on the earth's surface, and to thus fix definitely for that country both its "location" and its true "orientation".[1]

Perhaps it will not be inappropriate to interpolate here a remark on the basal structure of surveys of the earth's surface. There are two foundations of mapping. One method is that of fixing a number of points by astronomical observation. If this method is sufficiently elaborated, the whole surface, subject to the filling in of pictorial details, can be so dealt with. On the other hand, triangulation from one measured base can, as regards continuous, or nearly continuous, land surface, be adopted as a means to the same end. If an absolutely accurate base could be assured, and if an equally absolute accuracy could be attained in the instruments for ascertaining the angles of the triangulation derived from it, and if (what is even more problematical) the human observer could also be regarded as a stereotyped instrument, then (theoretically, at all events) the whole land surface of the world, except scattered islands far from continental areas, could be dealt with from the one base line. Thus either method may be regarded, in theory, as self-contained and complete. An example may be cited to show that accuracy can be obtained by triangulation. A century

[1] There will be found in the English edition of the *Petit Neptune Français*, published by William Faden (London, 1793, 4⁰), "A Table of the principal Places on the Coast of France, whose Situations of Latitude and Longitude have been determined by Astronomical Observation, by Messrs Maraldi and Cassini de Thury". They are 119 in number, classified as follows:—Towns, 84; Islands, 12; Forts and Towers, 11, and Light-Houses, 12.

At the end of the volume *La Méridienne de l'Observatoire Royal de Paris, vérifiée dans toute l'étendue du Royaume par de nouvelles Observations*, par Cassini de Thury (Paris, 1744, 4⁰), there is a *Table alphabétique des lieux qui ont été déterminés géométriquement par les Opérations de la Méridienne*. These places number 720.

ago the Lough Foyle base was measured in Ireland. It has never been re-measured, but an indirect test has been applied. The network of the principal triangulation connects the Lough Foyle base with the Salisbury Plain base, which was measured in 1849 with the same apparatus as that used in Ireland. If we assume that the latter base is errorless, the length of the former base, calculated through the triangulation, differs from the measured length by five inches, which is a minute difference in a base eight miles in length. The distance between the two bases is about 350 miles. It may also be of interest to refer to the table of comparison of the latitudes of thirty towns in France, (i) as fixed by observation, and (ii) as deduced by triangulation. This table is given by Cassini de Thury in his *Description Géométrique* referred to more particularly later. A third column shows the difference in each case.

In historical sequence the astronomical method was that first adopted, and is of great antiquity, and it is not till the sixteenth and seventeenth centuries of our era that any system of triangulation appears to have been thought of, and not till the eighteenth, and in France, that such a system was worked out in practice, and instruments were constructed which enabled it to be applied. It is not even then to be assumed that such instruments were available as would insure real scientific accuracy equivalent to that now attainable. In fact the difficulties arising from the imperfections of the instruments employed, mechanical and human, will be found translated in the great network of comparatively small triangles (more than 2000 in number) founded on eighteen bases, with which the Cassini map of the triangulation of France, dated in 1744, but corrected and completed in 1756, is crowded. Comparison may be made with the modern map of the triangulation of the British Isles issued by the Survey Department.[1]

[1] There is some apparent difficulty in establishing the exact chronology of the triangulation itself, and of the publication of the sheets of the resulting map of France.

The earliest map to show the triangles is that entitled *Nouvelle Carte qui comprend les principaux Triangles qui servent de Fondement à la Description Géométrique de la France. Levée par ordre du Roy. Par Messrs Maraldi et Cassini de Thury de l'Académie Royale des Sciences. Année* 1744. Upon it, in a panel headed "*Avertissement*", is a statement, too long to transcribe, explanatory of the operations employed. This—apparently the first—issue of the map gives a series of connected triangles following meridian lines, and lines perpendicular to the meridian, with others divergent from these two bases. They are said to number 400. This version of the map is found as a frontispiece or index map to the complete collection of the sheets constituting the map of France, when bound in three large folio volumes. It may be taken to represent the preliminary work carried out by the Académie des Sciences up to the year of its date.

Another version from the same plate, only altered by the filling in of a large number of additional triangles, so that the surface of the kingdom is almost uniformly covered by triangulation, is found in the volume entitled *Description Géométrique de la France* by Cassini de Thury, published in Paris in 1783, fol. This must be the final state of the map. In the *Projet et Acte d'Association* of 1756 published in the *Description Géométrique* a chain of more than 2000 triangles is referred to as having by then been established, and in the same work the author mentions 40,000 triangles as the number measured in establishing the details of the surface for the whole of France.

The engraving and publication of the sheets of the map itself date generally from 1756, only sheets 1 and 2 being so dated, and others bearing dates from that year to 1760. Only 22, however, out of the whole number of sheets bear any date. But impressions are extant of the first sheet of the series—that of Paris and the neighbourhood—clearly dated 1736. This, presumably, was a first and rather experimental engraving, though the same plate is subsequently used redated twenty years later, 1756. This early and isolated impression is singular, and has not been explained, or referred to, apparently, in any publication.

Section from the *Nouvelle Carte qui comprend les principaux Triangles qui servent de Fondement à la Description Géométrique de la France*, 1744.

The study historically of the Cassini survey of France shows that it combined the astronomical with the triangulation system. Of the Cassini family of astronomers and cartographers, and their work, the complete story has yet to be told. A considerable collection of materials, in view of the preparation of such a book as would do justice to the subject, was made by the late Ludovic Drapeyron more than thirty years ago (1896), and some original documents were then published; but, this author dying in 1901, no effort has since been made, as far as is known, to realize his proposals, which were based upon the author's interest in cartography alone. However, on other lines, Wolf's *Histoire de l'Observatoire de Paris*, published in 1902, does fill the gap, as far as astronomy and the personal history of the Cassini family are concerned, and leaves nothing to be desired on that side.

The first of this family, Jean Dominique (1625–1712), is generally stated in books of reference to have been appointed director of the Observatory of Paris upon its foundation in 1670; but, as a matter of fact, the Observatory of Paris did not come under the management of an actual director, formally appointed, until about a century later, when César François Cassini de Thury was, on November 12th, 1771, appointed, by *brevet*, Directeur Général. During the previous period the observatory had been regarded as belonging to the members of the Académie des Sciences, a corporate government naturally very prejudicial to regular progress in astronomical science. The foundation of the Greenwich Observatory was almost contemporaneous with that of Paris, five years later only, in 1675, with John Flamsteed as the first Astronomer Royal.

It may as well be recorded here that, on the death of Jean Dominique Cassini in 1712, he was succeeded by his son Jacques (1677–1756), who, in his turn, was followed by his son, César François Cassini, Comte de Thury (1714–84); this remarkable succession of eminent men being completed by the fourth in regular succession of this family, son of César François, Jean Dominique (1748–1845). This last of the astronomers of his family was arrested in 1794 (on February 13th) as a royalist, and tried by the revolutionary tribunal. He was fortunate enough to escape with his life, and to be able to relinquish his office and retire into comparative obscurity, but his escape was a very narrow one— his cousin, Mademoiselle de Forceville, who had taken refuge in his house in Paris and was arrested at the same time, being guillotined on the 6th June. Cassini himself was not liberated until the 5th August.

It is to the first two of the Cassinis that, as may have been already gathered, the astronomical foundations for the great map of France are to be attributed. To their two successors the work of the actual construction of the map— its cartographical execution—must be assigned.

For the present purpose astronomical progress may be marked, firstly, by the presentation to the King, Louis XIV, in 1682, on May 1st, during his first visit to the new observatory, of the results of the observations establishing the real cartographical boundaries of the kingdom of France; a presentation which drew from the King the exclamation: "Votre voyage m'a coûté une notable partie de mes états !"; secondly, by the laying out, in 1696, of the planisphere showing the positions of the thirty-nine localities fixed by the recent calculations, on the floor of the eastern saloon of the Observatory of Paris, already referred to; and thirdly, by the work of the second Cassini, in prolonging the meridian line of Paris south to the Canigou, a mountain at the eastern end of the chain of the Pyrenees, near the Spanish frontier (1700), and north to Dunkirk (1718).

The divergence of outline was very considerable. For instance, in the map of France, by Sanson, which has already been mentioned as having been presented to the Dauphin in 1679, Marseilles was placed several leagues too much to the south and Brest thirty leagues to the west, in the open sea.

Upon this foundation, with the measurement and co-ordination of the eighteen bases established throughout the kingdom, and the measurement, further, of the 400 principal triangles, the map of the triangulation of France could be completed for its publication in 1744.

This was the work of the third Cassini, and it was he, with the assistance of his son, who supervised and carried through to a conclusion the actual mapping and engraving of the whole of France, with the exception of a few sheets left unfinished upon the disorganization consequent on the Revolution of 1789, which were finally completed under the Republic and the Empire.

It was in 1744 that the third Cassini was in attendance on the King (Louis XV) during his campaign in the Low Countries, part of the operations of the War of the Spanish Succession, 1741–48. He was one of the engineers charged with the mapping of the country and the recording carto-graphically of the various military movements and under-takings. In this series of operations the Battle of Fontenoy, which took place on the 11th May, 1745, resulted in the surrender to the French under Marshal Saxe of a great part of the Low Countries, and this enabled Cassini to lay out a triangulation of the conquered area, and to construct the map which he annexed to his account of his work and experience in the second part of a quarto volume published in Paris in 1775, of which the first part is a *Relation d'un Voyage en Allemagne*, and the second a *Description des Conquêtes de Louis XV, depuis 1745 jusqu'en 1748*, a period of war terminated by the Peace of Aix-la-Chapelle, signed in October of the latter year.

The map above referred to is entitled: "*Carte des Pays Conquis par le Roy en 1744, 1745, et 1746. Levée Géométriquement Par Mr Cassini de Thury*". This map shows all the Low Countries as far north as Bergen-op-Zoom and Breda, with the triangulation adopted in its construction, and is supported in the text by complete and detailed figures for all these measurements. In the same volume, under the title noted above, extracted from an earlier publication (1765) is the account of an expedition made to carry the French triangulation into Germany, which contains similar plans and descriptive matter showing an important extension of cartographical exploration. Indeed, this volume is of the greatest value for the study of the methods and ideas of César François Cassini, which he sets out in a very ample and interesting manner.

But, to revert to the thread of the immediate narrative, and to the map of France. It was during the campaign in Flanders that an incident occurred critical in the history of cartographical endeavour. On July 7th, 1747, Cassini laid before the King, Louis XV, in the field, the different maps and plans he had completed to illustrate the military operations then in progress. The King was so well satisfied with this work that he, then and there, declared that the whole kingdom of France should be mapped in the same manner, confided the work to Cassini, and ordered the Controller-General of Finance to make the necessary arrangements. Thus the prosecution of this great project seemed to be definitely assured.

It was not so, however. The preparation of the maps themselves was not, it seems, definitely commenced until 1750 and a few years later (1756) Cassini was directed, on account of the poverty of the national exchequer, to discontinue his operations and dismiss the whole of his staff. What followed this unexpected blow to all his hopes is narrated by Cassini in the *Description Géométrique de la France*, published in 1783. The King was then at Compiègne. Cassini attended the court and presented to the King the sheet for that district (the second sheet of the map of France) which had just been printed off. His Majesty is said to have been astonished at the amount of detail delineated, especially in the forests, of which all the roads and avenues were shown, but he himself declared to Cassini that the map would have to be discontinued, to his great regret, for want of money. A discussion with the minister followed, in which Cassini urged upon him the disastrous effect of suspending operations in full execution and of disbanding the whole body of skilled surveyors and draughtsmen which had by then been built up—but without effect on his decision.

Thereupon Cassini had the courage to take upon himself the whole burden of this great enterprise, upon the condition that the King would support a scheme for forming an

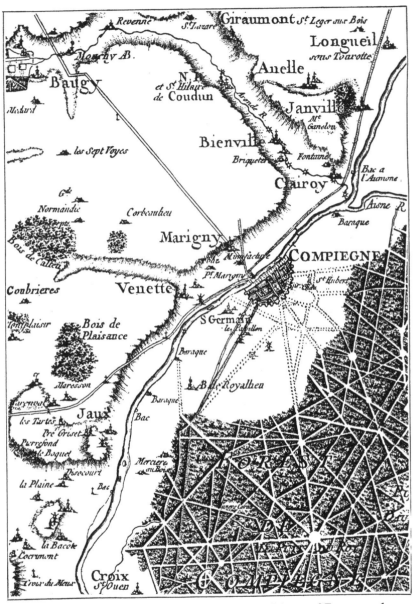

Section from Sheet 2 (Compiègne, etc.) of the Cassini map of France, 1756.

4-2

Association to attempt to raise by subscriptions and guarantees a sufficient sum to finance the completion of the 173 sheets of which the whole map was then estimated to consist. When the Association was launched, in 1756, it was stated that sixteen sheets of the map had been already published, and that, since the work of surveying for the detailed maps had been begun in 1750, a third of the work had been entirely completed. It was, at all events, so far advanced that it was possible to estimate with sufficient accuracy the cost per sheet at which the work could be finished.

This adventure was a remarkable success, the King having presented to the Association the whole of the material and instruments in use, and given to Cassini himself a list of the courtiers who had shown their willingness to join the Association as members. In a week's time fifty associates had come in, and the principal officers of the new body had been selected from men of distinction who undertook to discharge the duties assigned to them gratuitously. The Association was duly constituted on August 10th, 1756, under Articles which, as well as Cassini's "Projet de Souscription", are drawn with great clearness, and are of the utmost interest for the details they give of the whole of the proceedings and objects. They are marked throughout with the enthusiasm, honesty and practical ability which ornamented the career of César François Cassini throughout his whole life. As an inducement to subscribers to come in at once, it was provided that they should receive the earliest and best proof impressions of the sheets of the map in the order of priority of the inscription of their names on the register. The subscription was to close on October 1st, 1758, for France, and on January 1st, 1759, for abroad.

In the advertisements printed in an *Atlas Topographique et Militaire*, which was issued in Paris in 1758, by a well-known cartographical publisher, R. J. Julien, it is stated that he had been appointed agent for the sale of the map, both for France and for the other countries of Europe. The price is fixed at four livres the sheet, with a reduction to three livres five sous to subscribers for the whole set of 173 sheets. Julien adds, what is of considerable interest, a list of his correspondents in the principal cities of Europe outside France, which can be usefully compared with the list of subscribers to the *Atlas Universel* of the Robert de Vaugondys of the same period, already noted. It also appears, from Julien's advertisement, that the numbers of the sheets then published were 1–8, 21–27, 41–47, 60, 61, 80, 81, 83, 84, 93, 114, 125 and 126, or 32 sheets in all.

In a letter addressed to his co-associates by the fourth Cassini (Jean Dominique), and dated in 1801, it is stated that at the death of his father (César François) in 1784, there only remained unissued the province of Brittany. In 1793 there remained one sheet of that province to be engraved entirely, and two or three to complete. Finally, by the addition of nine sheets, or parts of sheets, on the coasts and land frontiers, the total was made up from the original 173 to an actual 182 sheets.

The work of the Association, all but finished, was paralysed during the revolutionary period, but the organization survived and its work was eventually achieved. It came to an end in 1818, when a final liquidation of seventeen shares in the hands of two surviving associates was arranged, on payment of the sum of 51,000 francs.

In this very year, the work of the "Carte de l'État Major"

commenced, but progress was very slow, and the first sheets
did not appear until 1833, the map being completed in 1878
only.

When all the sheets of the great Cassini map are assembled,
they make up, in the whole, a square of as nearly as possible
36 × 36 feet. The scale is 1 : 86,400, as compared with
our Ordnance Survey one-inch map, of which the scale is
1 : 63,360; Cassini's map being, therefore, on a lesser scale
of, approximately, 1⅜ miles to the inch. A reduction by
Louis Capitaine, one of the collaborators in the Cassini
survey, was published in 1789, in twenty-four sheets. This
is on a scale of 1 : 11,520, or on one of about 5 miles to the
inch, the scale of Cary's large map of England and Wales
of 1794, with which this reduction may, therefore, be con-
veniently compared.

The map shows all the usual details of the surface, roads,
rivers and canals, towns, villages and hamlets, with isolated
farms and abbeys, châteaux, with their gardens and parks,
woods and forests, vineyards, marshes, lakes and ponds,
wind and water mills, and crosses and gallows by the way-
side. The valleys of the rivers and streams are defined by
hill-shading of a uniform character; but this shading is no
further developed in the design of the surface, and, thus
limited, produces a defective appearance both in the technical and pictorial sense, so that the whole country, as
delineated, suggests a level plain of low elevation cut by
equally uniform shallow valleys throughout. This want of
representation of general surface irregularities is recognized
as the one striking defect in the system of cartographical
delineation adopted by Cassini. It was very literally followed
in England by the cartographer John Cary, in his first road-

book: *Cary's Actual Survey of the Great Post Roads between London and Falmouth*, published in 1784, and in some other of his early maps, but it does not appear to have been otherwise perpetuated. The actual design and detailed engraving are certainly very good work, and they mark an epoch in progress in these matters.

To realize the magnitude of the contribution to astronomical, geographical and cartographical science of the four Cassinis, the important volumes dealing with it historically, and with descriptions and details of their methods and instrumental appliances, should be read and studied; those of César François Cassini being of the most interest to cartographers. The titles of the principal of these publications will be found in the "List of Works of Reference" annexed, and they may be classed amongst the best sources of inspiration for the geographer and the cartographer. Amongst them, though it is only of collateral importance as regards cartography, the volume in which the fourth Cassini (Jean Dominique) describes his voyage from Le Havre to the French fishing settlement on the south coast of Newfoundland, with the return journey thence to the coast of Morocco, and to Cadiz and Brest, may be cited. This expedition was undertaken to test the new marine chronometers invented by Pierre Le Roy.

The account by César François Cassini of his important surveying expedition through the southern part of Germany is of special interest. In it he develops his ideas as to uniformity of scale, suggesting the adoption of such a scale for the mapping of the countries of Europe, a suggestion which foreshadowed the modern development represented by the world-map on the scale of one-millionth. His earlier work, *La Méridienne de l'Observatoire Royal de Paris*, published in 1744, and the *Description Géométrique de la France*, of 1783 (both already referred to), should be read by every student who wishes to obtain a real knowledge of the history of the science of cartography.

César François Cassini is, as an author, particularly interesting. One recognizes in his writings a very attractive personality, talented in a remarkable degree, and actuated by a complete devotion to the great work of his life, in which his success is associated with his own qualities of courage, energy and administrative ability, a great simplicity and an unselfish anxiety to achieve his scientific objects in the interests of his own nation and of the world's progress.

The publications attributable to the four astronomer members of this family are numerous. In the catalogue of the Bibliothèque Nationale, in Paris, where, it may be assumed, they are completely represented, the full number of titles is just over seventy, including, of course, pamphlets and minor works.

II

THE CARTOGRAPHICAL WORK OF THE
FRENCH ROAD SURVEYORS OF THE
EIGHTEENTH CENTURY

A<small>N</small> important, and indeed unique, cartographical work was undertaken in France during the eighteenth century, contemporaneously with the general survey of the Cassinis, but not directly associated with that survey. This was the complete and systematic mapping of the royal roads of the kingdom in connection with the reconstruction and reform of these roads, the chief part of which work seems to have been done in the period of about 1744 to 1776, the map of the triangulation of France bearing, it will be remembered, the date of the former year.

The reconstruction of the roads was based on the *corvée*, that is to say the *corvée royale*, superimposed, as a most oppressive burden, on that already borne by the peasantry of France in the form of the *corvée seigneuriale*, or manorial services. The counterpart of both these services existed in England, but, as there has never been developed in that country any centralized system of road repair and control, the provision of personal and team labour, organized as a purely parochial duty, was never there of a very oppressive character, and, no doubt in consequence, it survived much longer; indeed, until the coming into force of the Highway Act passed in 1835.

In France the labour exacted from the rural population was subject to the entirely arbitrary administration of a

Crown officer, the Intendant appointed as a fiscal officer and general administrator in each généralité. The corvée royale was abolished under Turgot's ministry in 1776, and, although, in the same year, the edict of abolition was revoked, it does not seem to have ever been again possible to reconstruct the system. It was finally abolished in 1787, just before the Revolution.

But it was upon this basis of forced labour, on a large scale, that the department set up for the purpose (that now known as the Ponts et Chaussées) was able to carry out the immense work of the reconstruction of the principal roads of France, and, incidentally, as one might say, to evolve a systematic delineation of the whole of these roads, together with the bordering area of the country, thus creating a cartographic work of the greatest interest and technical and artistic beauty, such as has never elsewhere, or at any time, been even attempted in the history of mankind.

The maps and plans, on a uniform scale, painted in water-colours, and bound up in généralités, still exist, in part, in the Archives Nationales, in Paris, in 65 atlas-folio volumes, these volumes containing what has survived of this immense and magnificent work. How much of it has been destroyed, or lost, it is not possible to say with any approach to exactitude. In 1786, it has been stated, there existed 2170½ sheets of these plans, representing 3135 leagues of roads, together with 804 sheets of drawings (plans and elevations) of bridges and culverts. In 1862, the number of road-plans had increased by 17½, but more than half of the drawings of bridges and other works had disappeared. What now remains, classified in the Archives Nationales, is of extraordinary interest to the cartographer, and, in a less degree, perhaps, to the student of history. These road-maps are drawn in horizontal strips in the upper half of each double sheet, leaving ample space below for notes and particulars, which, however, are found only on certain series and in little detail. The maps are in water-colour, and this coloration is, in general, in bright condition. The design is very fine and delicate, and the details shown are, in the first place, those of the great roads themselves, bordered with trees, and with indications of alterations proposed, the by-roads and paths, the rivers and brooks, with lakes and ponds. Of course, one finds also the centres of population, towns, villages and hamlets and even the *châteaux* with their parks, gardens and avenues, churches, monasteries, and farm buildings. The forests, heaths, and isolated trees add a great deal to the beauty of the general pictorial effect. Quarries are distinguished, the places where tolls have to be paid, wind and water mills, and the gallows and crosses on the roadside, are also drawn on the plans. Meadow land is in dark green, ploughed lands, vineyards and marshes are distinguished by special designs and tints, and the slopes of the hills and valleys are shown by a kind of hachure in brown. On the roads one sees the bridges and culverts and other indications including the mile-stones. The normal length of these strips is about 30, and the height about 12 inches.

In the library of the École des Ponts et Chaussées in Paris, there have also survived some of the volumes (eleven in all, as mentioned by Vignon in his *Études Historiques sur l'Administration des Voies Publiques en France*. Paris, 1862, tome II, at page 110), specially bound, of a series of plans, on one-half the original scale, of the principal roads leading from Paris to the frontiers of the kingdom, drawn by the most skilful draughtsman of the department, for the use of the King himself. A general map of the roads of France was also prepared, but it is not now known to exist. The only engraved and published example which can be referred to as illustrating this special art is a book of the road from Paris to Reims, prepared by a Benedictine monk, Dom Coutans, for the ceremonial journey of Louis XVI when he was crowned in the cathedral of the latter city in 1775. The maps here are carefully copied from the originals on the scale of one-half, and are engraved on a series of plates corresponding with the original sheets. A copy of this work, when coloured by hand, gives some idea of the beauty, art and technical value of the work of the engineers and draughtsmen employed on the originals from which it was reduced. It will be gathered that this special subject would repay a complete technical study. Here it can only be incidentally mentioned as an important part of the French cartography of the eighteenth century. The cartographical beginnings in this matter are not exactly established. The administrative effort to organize the roads of the kingdom under a central control dates from the appointment of the Duc de Sully as *Grand Voyer* by Henry IV in 1599, but the murder of that King (May 14th, 1610) put an end to progress, and it was half a century later under the administration of Colbert (but who died in 1683), appointed *Contrôleur Général des Finances* in 1661, the office of *Grand Voyer* being abolished, that the matter was again taken up with vigour. In 1716 only, was a real organization of the department now known as the Ponts et Chaussées achieved, and the *corvée des grands chemins* throughout the kingdom was not imposed on the people by royal decree until

June 13th, 1738, when the roads were classified under five divisions, and maps with descriptive particulars were directed to be made. It is from a little later, apparently, that the great work was actively pursued and continued for the period of at least thirty years, to which reference has already been made.

In respect of general road-maps of France, the matter is less clear. The very large manuscript map of France which is preserved in the library of the Ministry of War, in Paris, has already been referred to. In this map the roads and rivers are quite a special feature. There may possibly be other general maps of the same character in existence, but none appear to have been described up to the present time. The map is interesting as being on practically the same scale as Saxton's general map of England and Wales, of about 1584, dealt with in the first section of chapter I, and it is comparable, in the matter of roads, with Lea's version of the latter map of 1687, with which it is no doubt approximately contemporaneous.

As early as 1679 orders are found directing in particular cases the construction of maps of the roads, but I have not discovered any examples of this work before 1714, the year in which it appears that the Intendants of all the généralités were directed to send in plans of the royal roads, with estimates of the expense of maintenance and repair. A few examples of the original reports and maps still exist, all dated in 1714.

Nothing more seems to be known of this character, although it is probable that such reports were from that time annually rendered, until the maps ordered in 1738 began to appear, as they are now found brought together in the

Archives Nationales in Paris. In the later stages of the work of the surveyor, sketch maps seem to have been drawn, as perhaps they may have been, as a general practice, without the survival of examples. Of these also a small number, at all events, relating to roads in the Morbihan, in Brittany, have survived.

III

THE MAP OF THE BELGIAN PROVINCES OF THE COMTE DE FERRARIS

No study of the cartography of the eighteenth century would be complete without reference to what is, perhaps, the most magnificent work of the kind ever undertaken, prior to the great governmental surveys of modern times.

This is the map known as the *Carte de Cabinet*, a map of the Austrian possessions in the Low Countries, constructed under the direction of the Lieutenant-General Comte Joseph de Ferraris, in the period 1770–78, for the Austrian Government. Its title is *Carte des provinces autrichiennes, de la principauté de Liége et Stavelot, de quelques enclaves de l'Empire et de la Hollande, et des franchises qui s'y trouvent renfermées*. It consists of 275 sheets, drawn and coloured with great care by hand, seven different colours being used, and on a scale of 1 : 11,520. When put together these sheets make up a map of 98½ feet in width, by 65½ feet in height. Only three copies were made, one for the Emperor of Austria, another for the Vienna Foreign Office, and the third for the Brussels Government. Each sheet had a descriptive memoir —these memoirs, in manuscript, making up twelve volumes of 4108 pages in all.

When the Austrian archducal administration withdrew from the Low Countries in 1794, the copy of the map of Ferraris in their possession was taken away, but, in accordance with the provisions of the Treaty of Saint Germain-en-Laye (1919), the Belgian Government claimed the restoration of this map, with other documents, and it is now in the Bibliothèque Royale, at Brussels.

The survey was carried out in sections of a square league each, giving, in all, 4250 of these sections. The work is of extraordinary detail and beauty. It shows, for instance, with such accuracy the areas of woodlands that it is possible to-day to make an exact comparison of these areas in every part of the maps with the conditions now subsisting as delineated on the modern government maps. The roads are shown also in detail, and the memoirs, which consist of an exact examination of each region, give full particulars of the ways of communication and their structural character for each sheet. The paved highways, of which in 1715 only 61 kilomètres existed, had been increased to 925 kilomètres in 1794 at the close of the Austrian rule. This progress may be brought into comparison with that in France in the same period to which attention has already been drawn. Voltaire, writing in 1750, says: "De toutes les nations modernes, la France et le petit pays des Belges sont les seuls qui aient des chemins dignes de l'antiquité", which must be allowed to be justified by the facts of the case. As a general rule these roads had been built up in the second half of the eighteenth century by the governments of the different provinces, and it was the provinces which remained responsible for their repair and maintenance.

A reduction of the *Carte de Cabinet* was undertaken and was engraved in 1777. This was distinguished as the *Carte Marchande*, as it was placed on sale (in April, 1778), and copies are now not uncommon. It is in twenty-five sheets, on a scale of 1 : 86,400, that is to say on the same scale as Cassini's great map of France, with which it is thus associated, and is a beautiful example of the cartographic art of the period. The title is *Carte Chorographique des Pays-Bas Autrichiens*, 1777. It was engraved by L. A. Dupuis. In scale it approximates to the British inch to the mile Ordnance Survey Map, as the *Carte de Cabinet* may be said to do to the 6-inch map. This reduction measures rather more than 12 feet in width by 9 feet in height.

Perhaps the most remarkable, and indeed unique feature of the Ferraris survey, was the preparation of the descriptive memoir annexed to each sheet, minutely describing the character of the surface and the economic condition of the provinces of Belgium. There is first mentioned the principal town and other towns of any importance. The geographical situation is described. Their origin, and their civil and military history is added, with an account of all operations of war which have occurred within the area of the sheet in question. The geology, the character of the surface relief, the nature of the soil, the condition of agriculture, the different species of timber and other trees, the cultivations, the agricultural and pastoral produce, the wastes and marsh lands are all dealt with. In the same way the industrial and commercial situation is examined, the number and kind of mills, forges and manufactories and their local situation are passed in review. Then the whole question of ways of communication on land and water, with the water-courses, canals and lakes is studied in detail. And finally, very complete notes giving valuable information with regard to military movements and manœuvres are added.

This is in fact an elaborate *Regional Survey* to which anything now being attempted here, or elsewhere, appears quite insignificant. It is in view of these details, apparently, that the Austrians, retreating before the French invaders in 1794, took the very proper precaution, from a military point of view, of removing the Brussels copy of both the map and the attached memoirs. As a matter of fact the first thing the French did, on reaching Brussels, was to seize all copies of the engraved reduction, as well as the copper plates themselves—transporting the latter to Paris, where they were utilized for further impressions of this map.

It will be realized from the above summary what is the extraordinary local historical importance both of the map of Ferraris and of the memoirs annexed, and generally of this unusual association of graphic delineation of surface and full descriptive text.

What is known of the life of the Comte de Ferraris is not without interest. The difficulties he had to meet in his cartographical work were chiefly financial, comparable with those experienced by the Cassinis in France, and, in a lesser degree, by the promoters and supporters of the surveys of England, both in the Elizabethan period, and in modern times in connection with the British Ordnance Survey itself —at least in the early stages of its existence; but Ferraris had the advantage of being personally a favourite of the

Empress Maria Theresa, and he was thus able to overcome, in the end, the objections raised by the ministers in Vienna to the expenditure involved, and to bring his work to a speedy and satisfactory issue, and incidentally to establish for himself a magnificent monument in the progress of the world's cartographical history.[1]

[1] The career of Ferraris being almost exclusively a military one does not quite fall within the limits of this work. Nevertheless, it may be admitted at least in outline as a note.

Comte Joseph de Ferraris was born at Lunéville, in Lorraine, on the 20th April, 1726, where his family had been settled from the beginning of the seventeenth century. It came originally from Piedmont. In 1735 he entered the Austrian court as page to the Empress Amelia, widow of Joseph I (1678–1711) and aunt of Maria Theresa, afterwards Empress-Queen, whose liking for Ferraris probably dates from this period when she would have known him, then little more than a child, she herself being as a young woman at the height of her beauty, which is said to have been remarkable.

Ferraris devoted himself very early to the study of the exact sciences and more particularly to that of mathematics. He entered the Austrian army in 1741 as ensign. Having been wounded at the battle of Czaslau the 17th May, 1742, where he served brilliantly, he was promoted lieutenant, and before the end of the campaign he received the command of a company of infantry. In 1750 he was promoted major and in 1757 lieutenant-colonel.

On the 14th October, 1758, at the battle of Hochkirchen, he captured a battery of cannon, at the head of the regiment of Charles of Lorraine, of which he was colonel, and for this exploit he received the cross of the order of Maria Theresa, which the empress had just instituted. Having been further promoted to general-major in 1761, he was appointed director general of the artillery in the Austrian Netherlands.

Appointed lieutenant-general in 1773, and governor of Termonde in 1775, at the commencement of the war with Prussia, in 1778, he received very flattering evidence of the confidence of Maria Theresa, who placed under his direction the young archduke Maximilian.

During the reign of Joseph II (1780–90) the general was sent into Belgium during the revolution in Brabant, and he took command of the Austrian army after the troops under General d'Alton had been forced to evacuate Brussels.

It may be mentioned also that attention has only quite recently been drawn to the former existence of another considerable work by Ferraris, namely, that of the mapping and description in detail of the Crown Forests of the county of Namur. An inventory of the sheets of the map and of the relative documents has been discovered, but nothing more seems now to exist of these important historical materials.

After the death of the Emperor Joseph II, Ferraris continued to be held in high esteem by the succeeding Austrian emperors.

In 1793, in spite of his 67 years, he took an active part in the campaign against France; he commanded an army corps and distinguished himself particularly in the engagements of Saultain and Tamars, as well as at the siege of Valenciennes, and was rewarded first with the ribbon and, shortly afterwards, with the grand cross of the order of Maria Theresa.

At the end of this campaign the Emperor recalled him to Vienna and appointed him vice-president of the Council of War. He became field marshal in 1807, and died at Vienna 1st April, 1814, universally regretted. One of his biographers says that "he united with uncommon talents, suavity of manner, an exquisite politeness and perfect loyalty". He had married Henriette, daughter of the Duke d'Ursel, by whom he had one daughter Maria Wilhelmine, born 3rd September, 1780, and who married Count Franz Zichy, the 6th May, 1799. She died the 25th January, 1866. [Translation from the *Bulletin de la Société Royale Belge de Géographie*, 1891. Brussels, 1891. 8°.]

CHAPTER IV

British Cartography of the Second Half of the Eighteenth Century, its Connection with the Triangulation of France, and the Ordnance Survey

I

JOHN CARY AND HIS WORK

JOHN CARY may be taken as a representative of another stage in the evolution of the art of map construction, and of another approach towards the exactness of the officially approved maps of our own times. He was certainly very much influenced by the method of map delineation and of surface representation adopted by Cassini. This will be clear to anyone who compares any sheet of the map of France with the road maps in Cary's *Road to Falmouth*, published in 1784, his first publication in the nature of a road-book, and with other of his maps of that period.

As he built up the important cartographical establishment, which was continued by his sons until as late as 1850, he had many rivals, the times lending themselves to the growth of working cartography, but he can well be particularly admired, for his art, his energy, and his business aptitude, and it is to him and to his work that attention is directed in this section.

Cary came, apparently, of a Wiltshire family, of the town, or neighbourhood, of Warminster, and in 1770 he is found

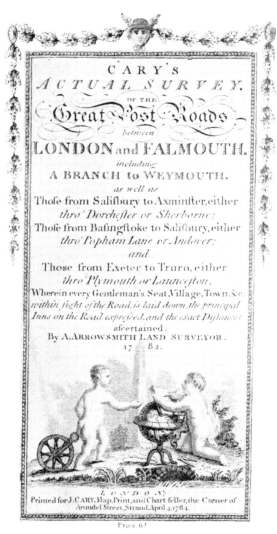

CARY'S
ACTUAL SURVEY,
OF THE
Great Post Roads
between
LONDON and FALMOUTH,
including
A BRANCH to WEYMOUTH,
as well as
Thofe from Salifbury to Axminfter, either
thro' Dorchefter or Sherborne;
Thofe from Bafingftoke to Salifbury, either
thro' Popham Lane or Andover;
and
Thofe from Exeter to Truro, either
thro' Plymouth or Launcefton,
Wherein every Gentleman's Seat, Village, Town, &c.
within fight of the Road, is laid down, the principal
Inns on the Road expreffed, and the exact Diftances
afcertained.
By A. ARROWSMITH LAND SURVEYOR.
17 82.

LONDON,
Printed for J. CARY, Map, Print, and Chart-feller, the Corner of
Arundel Street, Strand, April 4, 1784.

Price 6ˢ

Title-page of *Cary's Actual Survey of the*
Great Post Roads between London and Falmouth, 1784.

apprenticed, for seven years, with a premium of £30, to William Palmer, of New Street Square, London, engraver. No doubt it was this William Palmer who engraved a number of maps in the period 1766–98, and, if so, the association would explain Cary's early, and even exclusive, devotion to map engraving. Two years later his younger brother, Francis, was also apprenticed to an engraver, for a like term, and for the same premium. Francis was associated with his brother in his business, probably for many years, but there is little known of his personal work or ability.

John Cary appears to have married in 1779, two years after the expiration of his apprenticeship. He died in Chelsea in August, 1835, being described as of 81 years of age. He must thus have been born about 1754, and was apprenticed when sixteen years of age. Francis Cary died in 1836, aged 80. The eldest brother, George, of this family was a haberdasher in the Strand; the youngest, William, was well known as a scientific instrument maker, and was associated with John Cary in the production of globes, a part of his cartographical work. William was a pupil of Jesse Ramsden, whose work for the early trigonometrical survey has been mentioned, and will be further referred to more fully later. The Carys were energetic and prosperous people, and John must have been at his death a comparatively rich man.

Throughout his long artistic and business career, even if we judge only from his immense output of atlases, maps and charts, geological maps and tables, road-maps, road-books and itineraries, town plans, canal, dock and drainage plans, miscellaneous publications, and terrestrial and celestial globes, extending over a period of about half a century, the formidable total justifies us in regarding him as a remarkable exponent of the art and method of cartography. His direct descendants are still known, and the family pedigree can be very completely traced, in the descending order.

It is probable that Cary engraved maps during his apprenticeship, and several undated canal plans are known which bear his name as engraver, and in one case based on a survey made as early as 1769. These plans, and others of later dates, were published in connection with the construction of the canal system of commercial communication in England which began in 1759, when the Act of Parliament for making the Bridgewater Canal, in Lancashire, was passed, and continued until the advent of railways in the third decade of the following century put a stop to this work by the introduction of a formidable and all-absorbing rival. A plan dated 1779, and bearing "J. Cary *sculpt.*", is the earliest of such engravings which can, with certainty, be ascribed to Cary, but in the two following years his signature appears on a set of maps and plans, thirty-eight in number, on thirty-two plates, illustrating the two large quarto volumes of a work entitled, *The Field of Mars*, of which the first edition appeared in 1781. The plates are variously dated between August, 1780, and August, 1781.

In this latter year Cary engraved a small map of Europe; in 1783, associated with a publisher named Wallis, he produced a single sheet map of the environs of London and a pocket map of the metropolis and, also, for another publisher, a chart of the British Channel.

By this time Cary had established, by these successful cartographical engravings, his talent and capacity in this art, and he is now found established in his own name and in his own place of business, where his subsequent activity was continuous and successful, and his output always increasing in volume and importance.

It is to be observed that while Cary started in business life as a working engraver, he almost immediately launched out as a publisher, and that he also undertook the survey of land, as is shown by an advertisement issued in 1790, in which he describes himself as a Land Surveyor: "*Estates surveyed and planned with Accuracy and Dispatch*". In a similar connection he carried out for the Government a complete and accurate measurement of the roads of England and Wales, the first undertaken since that of John Ogilby of 1675, a measurement which has only within the last few years been repeated for the purpose of the Road Board, and to enable the roads of the country to be, for the first time, regularly classified for centralized supervision and the distribution of grants in aid from the National Exchequer.

In this operation he employed five surveyors, who measured in all, according to Cary's statements, upwards of 10,000 miles of roadway, the measurement being made, as was the case of that undertaken by John Ogilby more than a century earlier, with the perambulator or odometer, a wheel pushed before the surveyor, which, in its revolutions, ticked off the distance run on a dial fixed in the framework.

Cary's engagement to survey the post roads was made in 1794, for 9000 miles, and this work he had completed, apparently, in time for its incorporation in the first edition of *Cary's New Itinerary*, a well-known work, which ran, in rivalry with Daniel Paterson's *New and Accurate Description* (1771–1832), from 1798 to 1828.

But the first of Cary's road-books was one which is now

rare—that of the *Great Post Roads between London and Falmouth*, a series of beautifully engraved little road-maps, from a survey by Aaron Arrowsmith made in 1782, and itself published by Cary in 1784. If these maps are examined and compared with the art and technique of surface representation of Cassini's map of France, it will be seen, as has been already suggested, that the inspiration of the latter great work had crossed the Channel, and largely influenced Cary's methods.

Amongst Cary's atlases, the *New and Correct English Atlas* is the earliest, appearing in 1787. It was a quarto atlas of the English counties. Eight re-issues are known up to 1831, followed by several editions from the same plates by G. F. Cruchley. The small octavo set of county maps, with the title, the *Traveller's Companion*, was published in 1790, with a long succession of editions till as late as 1828. The *New English Atlas* was a large folio set of the counties, 1809 to 1834, and similarly continued by Cruchley. A year earlier than this last publication, in 1808, appeared a large folio general atlas, the *New Universal Atlas*, of which there are several successive reprints.

It seems probable that Cary drew the designs of his county maps, as well as that of his first large general map of England and Wales (1794), from the materials supplied by the large-scale county maps, surveyed and engraved for different publishers during the latter half of the eighteenth century. This work, though wanting in uniformity, and in many cases in accuracy, involved a distinct advance on anything in the nature of original cartography which had been undertaken in this country since the Elizabethan survey of Christopher Saxton. It was encouraged by the Society of

Arts, which in 1759 offered a prize, or premium, of £100 for the map of any county on the scale of an inch to a mile, the first actual award being made to Benjamin Donn, who, in 1765, received £100 for his map of Devonshire, engraved by Thomas Jefferys. Maps continued to be produced, and awards of money and of gold and silver medals continued to be made, until as late as 1809, by which time upwards of forty-one county maps had appeared. Of these three were engraved by John Cary: one of Oxfordshire (1797), another of Glamorganshire (1799), and a third, for which a gold medal was awarded, of Cardiganshire (1804). The financial support to these undertakings given by the Society of Arts was little more than complimentary, and they depended for their success on subscriptions by landowners and residents in the respective counties, whose seats and names were given prominence on the maps themselves. It resulted from this system that the counties deficient in resident gentry were not surveyed, and this want of local financial support appears to account for the absence of thirteen out of the fifty-two counties of England and Wales from the list of the large-scale maps of this period. The expenditure on survey and engraving of such maps was considerable. In the case of a projected map of Sussex, mentioned by Richard Gough, the map was to be published in eight large sheets, on a scale of two inches to the mile, and it was estimated to cost more than £2400 for surveying, drawing and engraving, and to take six years in execution. Four hundred subscriptions, at six guineas each for the whole map, were asked for.

Taken as a whole, these undertakings are remarkable as exhibiting both public spirit and commercial and technical enterprise in cartography in England during the half-century immediately preceding the commencement of the work of Government and systematic survey of the whole country.

Of Cary's general maps, that of England and Wales and part of Scotland, in 81 sheets, on a scale of 5 miles to the inch, published in 1794, is perhaps the most important. Of this there was a reduction on a scale of 15 miles to the inch in 1796, in a single sheet, of which numerous re-issues are known.

Cary engraved, besides, the very fine *New Map of the County of Oxford* in 1797, as already noticed, in sixteen sheets, with a large-scale inset plan of the city filling two of the sheets, and a large map of Russia, in four sheets, published in 1814, which is an important piece of work, and is apparently extremely rare. In 1818 he published a six-sheet map of England and Wales and part of Scotland; in 1824, *A New Map of Hindostan*, in six sheets, of which a second issue appeared in 1829, with a new inset map of *The Burman Empire* engraved in the right-hand bottom corner.

Finally, there appeared an *Improved Map of England and Wales, with a considerable portion of Scotland*, in 65 sheets. This is dated 1832, and must have been founded on what had then appeared of the Ordnance Survey one-inch map, reduced to one-half that scale. Cruchley in his reprint of about 1852 describes it, relatively to the latter, as being of "half the scale and half the price".

William Smith's geological maps and sections were all published by John Cary. They appeared between 1815 and 1819–24. A great number of road-books and maps were issued from his press, as well as many canal plans, and maps of London and the neighbourhood were also numerous as products of his cartographical activity. He was a maker of globes, both terrestrial and celestial, on a large scale, being associated in this work with his brother William.

This enumeration gives only a slight idea of Cary's output. It is completely catalogued in a study of this carto-grapher, published in 1925 by the Cambridge University Press, which may be referred to.[1]

Endeavour has been made to arrive at a statistical sum-mary of this output, but without much success. There is an essential difficulty in such a numerical computation, on account of the want of a settled unit upon which the carto-bibliographer can work. If an atlas is regarded as a unit, viewed as a book, the matter is comparatively a simple one, but it may well be argued that the individual maps it con-tains are to be counted separately. Then there are maps made up of a large number of sheets, each surrounded with a border, and the question in that case arises whether the map is one thing, or is to be regarded and counted according to the number of such sheets. A road-book made up of a long series of separate plates of roads presents the same problem, and there are other difficulties of the same nature. This is, in fact, a carto-bibliographical puzzle to which attention may well be called.

It seems that the general atlases published by Cary contain about 550 individual maps. Perhaps it would not be rash to estimate, on the lowest scale of method suggested above, an output of 1000 maps, books and other publications. At all events it was very large indeed, and continuous, with re-issues and reprints over half a century at least, while

[1] *John Cary, Engraver, Map, Chart and Print-Seller and Globe-Maker, 1754 to 1835.* Cambridge, 1925. 8º.

some of the material accumulated has been made use of in various forms of publication up to our own time, the whole constituting a monument to the ability and energy of this British cartographer, in many ways a pioneer in the art and science he adorned.

II

GENERAL WILLIAM ROY AND THE EARLY HISTORY OF THE ORDNANCE SURVEY

I T may not be inappropriate to close this historical summary of cartographical progress with some slight account of the early history and origin of the British Ordnance Survey, which links itself up naturally with the great initiative in exact survey and triangulation of the Cassinis in France.

For this purpose the charming volume *The Early Years of the Ordnance Survey*, written by Sir Charles Close, and published by the Institute of Royal Engineers in 1926, a work to be warmly recommended to all students of cartography, has been largely drawn upon.

The account given by William Roy of the circumstances in which appears to lie the germ of the Survey as we now know it, is found in the *Philosophical Transactions of the Royal Society for 1785*. Roy says:

The rise and progress of the rebellion which broke out in the Highlands of Scotland in 1745, and which was finally suppressed by His Royal Highness the Duke of Cumberland at the battle of Culloden in the following year, convinced the Government of what infinite importance it would be to the State that a country, so very inaccessible by nature, should be thoroughly explored and laid open, by establishing military posts in its inmost recesses, and carrying roads of communication to its remoter parts. With a view to the commencement

South-East Terminal of the Hounslow Heath Base, measured
by General William Roy in 1784.

of arrangements of this sort, a body of infantry was encamped at Fort Augustus in 1747, under the command of the late Lord Blakeney, at that time a Major-General, at which camp my much respected friend, the late Lieut.-General Watson, then Deputy Quarter-Master General in North Britain, was officially employed. This officer, being himself an Engineer, active and indefatigable, a zealous promoter of every useful undertaking, and the warm and steady friend of the industrious, first conceived the idea of making a map of the Highlands. As Assistant Quarter-Master, it fell to my lot to begin, and afterwards to have a considerable share in, the execution of that map; which being undertaken under the auspices of the Duke of Cumberland, and meant at first to be confined to the Highlands only, was nevertheless at last extended to the Lowlands; and thus made general in what related to the main-land of Scotland, the islands (excepting some lesser ones near the coast) not having been surveyed.

This map has never been engraved, and Roy describes it as "having been carried out with instruments of the common, or even inferior kind, and the sum allowed for it being inadequate to the execution of so great a design in the best manner, it is rather to be considered as a magnificent military sketch, than a very accurate map of a country".

Sir Charles Close thus summarizes its character:

The work is clearly an elaborate compass sketch, the roads and some of the streams have been paced, and the mountains have been put in roughly by the eye. Near the towns the work is carefully drawn. Cultivation is indicated by open diagonal hatching. The hill features are shown by rough, faint, brush, sepia shading or *hachuring*; the larger mountains are shown by similar, only darker, shading....

The scale of the map is apparently intended to be 1000 yards to one inch, or 1 : 36,000, a scale which was never again adopted for official maps in this country.

A reduction in a single sheet was made by Roy and was engraved and published in 1774.

Roy was born in 1726, and he held a long series of appointments in, or connected with, the army. In 1765 he was appointed, having then reached the army rank of Deputy Quarter-Master General, Surveyor-General of Coasts, and Engineer for making and directing Military Surveys in Great Britain, and for the discharge of these duties he was assigned pay at the rate of 20s. a day, which allowance continued until his death. He was elected a Fellow of the Royal Society in 1767. He died suddenly in London, in July, 1790, whilst occupied in correcting the proofs of a paper for the Royal Society. His life was throughout one of continuous activity in surveying and in the study of everything relating thereto, so that he may be regarded as the most notable figure in the period of development of cartography in this country up to the time of the actual foundation of the Ordnance Survey, a few years after his death.

Wars, including that with America, very largely obstructed his persistent efforts to secure the systematic mapping of the British Isles, and it was not till quite the close of his life that opportunity was given for the display of his talents and great accumulated experience in carrying through a substantial work tending to that object. This opportunity was associated with the suggestion of the French Government, prompted by Jean Dominique Cassini, the fourth of the family, acting for his father César François Cassini de Thury, whose life and work have already been dealt with and who at this time was disabled by ill health (he died September 4th, 1784, and was then succeeded as Director of the Observatory of Paris by his son), that the triangulation of France should be extended across the Straits of Dover so as to establish the exact relative positions of the great national observatories of Paris and Greenwich. This application took the form of a *mémoire* by Cassini, which was received by the Government and transmitted to the Royal Society in October, 1783. The King himself (George III) took a personal interest in these proposals, and defrayed the cost of the necessary instruments for measuring a base and laying out the triangles involved in the operations contemplated, and for this purpose the services of Major-General Roy were lent by the military authorities.

Sir Charles Close sums up the situation at this moment in the following terms:

At the time of the Peace of 1783 there was in Great Britain no systematic triangulation, if we except the little, rough work that Roy himself had carried out in Scotland. Although the plane-table, in practically its modern form, had been known for at least two hundred years, it appears that all the official sketches and reconnaissances were executed with the magnetic compass, and the order of accuracy was just that of a military compass sketch. Roy's intention to stiffen up Watson's map of Scotland (that of 1747 already referred to) with a trigonometrical frame-work, had never been carried into effect. His efforts to establish a national survey department had been put aside, as a consequence, first of the Seven Years' War, and later of the war with America. The maps of this country were due to private effort and were inferior in accuracy to those produced by Major Rennell in Bengal. Neither in geodesy nor in topography had our great-grandfathers any reason to be content with the state of affairs at home.

This then was the general situation when the question of the measurement of a base and the triangulation therefrom, in order to connect with the completed triangulation of France, was raised officially, and steps were taken to give effect to the arrangement with the French authorities.

It was first necessary to measure a base in the south of England, and Hounslow Heath was selected for this purpose. This base was measured in 1784. It was originally intended to measure it by means of deal rods, which was then the almost universal custom on the continent, and a set of them was made for the purpose, but these were found to vary in length according to the humidity of the atmosphere, and the length of the base was actually determined by the use of glass tubes, about an inch in diameter, one of them being no less than twenty-six feet in length.

The length of this base, after applying corrections for temperature and reduction to sea-level, was 27,404·01 feet. Re-measured, after Roy's death, in 1791, with two chains made by Ramsden, the value was found to be 27,404·24 feet. In 1858 the length was again determined and then found to be 27,406·19 feet. In Roy's time the terminals of the Hounslow Heath base were wooden pipes a foot in diameter. In 1791 they were found to be decayed, and were replaced by guns fixed vertically with the muzzle upwards.

In the paper of which Roy was correcting the proofs at the time of his death, he advocates strongly the use of in-destructible terminals. He says, "These should be low circular buildings, rising but a few feet above the surface of the Heath, composed of the hardest materials such as granite.... They would resemble those basements of ancient crosses we often meet with". His idea has not been adopted, but, as a memorial to commemorate the 200th anniversary of General Roy's birth, a tablet was affixed in

1927 to each of the two terminals to commemorate his services, and that on the South-East Terminal was unveiled by the Astronomer Royal (Sir Frank Dyson) on the 22nd February in that year.

The further proceedings in the triangulation were much retarded by the delay in the construction of a theodolite sufficiently accurate for taking the angles, and it was not until the 31st July, 1787, that the new and very elaborate instrument was delivered and placed on the station at the south-east end of the base. At this time Roy was engaged in measuring a second base in Romney Marsh, a base measured with a hundred-feet steel chain made by Ramsden, laid in wooden troughing. The length came out at 28,535·7 feet. As deduced from the Hounslow base there was a difference of 2·4 feet, or about one in 12,000, though Roy himself seems to have thought that the difference was less than a foot.

On the 23rd September, 1787, he received the visit of Jean Dominique Cassini at Dover. In the library of the Observatory of Paris there still exists, written in a beautifully clear and neat hand, the Journal kept by Cassini of his journey from Paris to Dover, and the return to the French coast after having arranged with General Roy and his colleagues the details of the operations to be carried out across the Channel for establishing the connection between the triangulations in the two countries. Cassini, accompanied by MM. Méchain and Legendre, embarked on the 23rd September at Calais, on an English boat, and reached Dover about mid-day.

Cassini writes in warm terms of General Roy, who, with Dr Blagden, received the French visitors, and the whole party seem to have arrived at an immediate and cordial understanding as to the work to be taken in hand.

The stations on the French coast were to be at Dunkirk, Calais, Blanc Nez, and Mont Lambert, north of Boulogne, at which lights were to be exhibited for observation from Dover and several other stations on the English coast. On the 25th the French party, with Dr Blagden, crossed the Channel to Boulogne, and the operations commenced on the 29th.

The agreement between the distances across the Channel derived from the English and French triangulations respectively was very close, the actual discrepancy being seven feet in the distance between Dover Castle and the spire of the church of Notre Dame in Calais, the Hounslow Heath base alone being used on this side of the Channel. The distance between the two points is slightly over 26 miles.

No angles observed by Roy are incorporated in the great triangulation finally adopted for the survey of the British Islands,

But [to again quote Sir Charles Close] Roy's work deserves all praise. It was the first accurate triangulation carried out in this country and set a remarkably high standard; it amply fulfilled its original scientific purpose; it provided for the first time, a thoroughly reliable frame-work for map-making, and it led directly to the formal founding of the Ordnance Survey.

It was not, however, till a year after Roy's death that the Survey was officially founded, and began the work it has pursued ever since.

The official date of the constitution of the Ordnance Survey is July 10th, 1791, and from that time for the next thirty-three years the object of the survey was definitely the production of a one-inch map of the United Kingdom. The various larger-scale maps and plans followed. It does not come within the scope of this work to deal with them, but of the first maps issued on the one-inch scale notice may be taken here, as they are of historical interest.

Amongst the large-scale county maps already referred to several were published by William Faden, who had at this time a considerable business and reputation in the engraving and production of maps, and it was to this publisher that the Survey, being at that time unprovided with the necessary staff of engravers, confided the production of the first sheets of the one-inch map—being four in number, forming a complete map of Kent, with part of Essex. This map was published on the first day of the new century, January 1st, 1801. It is engraved on copper, and the sheets are about 33½ inches by 22½ inches. The title runs: "General Survey of England and Wales, an Entirely New and Accurate Survey of the County of Kent with Part of the County of Essex. Done by the Surveying Draughtsmen of His Majesty's Honourable Board of Ordnance, on the basis of the Trigonometrical Survey". The dedication is dated "Drawing Room, Tower, January 1st, 1801". The engraving is a very satisfactory piece of work, recalling the design of the large-scale county maps already referred to, in being engraved over the whole surface with a conventional indication of the cultivation and field enclosures, borrowed, probably, from the conventional methods found pretty generally in these maps, but not further adopted by the Survey. The hill shading follows somewhat that of John Cary.

No other sheets of these maps appeared until more than four years later, when the Survey undertook the engraving and publication from their office in the Tower of London. The map then issued was that of Essex, and it differed somewhat from the methods of surface delineation used by Faden, the map having now reached its final form, which has not since varied. The title is: "Part the First of the General Survey of England and Wales, done by the Surveyors of His Majesty's Ordnance under the direction of Lieut.-Colonel Mudge of the Royal Artillery, F.R.S.". This map also is in four sheets, of practically the same dimensions as those of Faden's Kent. It has the imprint: "Published April 18th, 1805, by Lieut.-Colonel Mudge, Tower. Engraved at the Tower".

In justice to the surveyors in charge of the Ordnance Survey in Ireland in the early part of the last century, attention should be drawn to the memoirs proposed to be published for each parish in that country, but which, unfortunately, never got beyond that issued in 1837 for the parish of Templemore, co. Londonderry. This volume gives an account of the topography, geology, botany and zoology of the parish; a description of the city of Londonderry and a history of the town-lands of the whole parish; with a third section dealing with statistics, social economy and manufactures. It contains a large number of plans and other illustrations.

If this magnificent scheme had been carried out, it would have been comparable, as an example of Regional Survey, to the *mémoires* of the Ferraris map of the Low Countries to which reference has been made.

The work was discontinued on financial grounds, but the manuscript remains are still preserved in the library of the Royal Irish Academy in Dublin. These papers are contained in fifty boxes, and relate to nineteen out of the thirty-two Irish counties; the counties of Antrim and Londonderry accounting for thirty-seven of these boxes.

In the "Preliminary Notice" to the Templemore volume, Thomas Colby, then Colonel R.E., and super-intendent of the Survey in Ireland, makes an observation which is well worth consideration even now:

It is scarcely necessary to remark that a map is in its nature but a part of a Survey, and that much of the in-formation connected with it can only be advantageously embodied in a memoir, to which the map then serves as a graphic index.

CONCLUSION

A WORK of the kind now attempted, being compiled from a large number of sources of materials and reduced to a very condensed form, seems hardly to require anything in the nature of a summary, but it may be well to review, in a few words, the historical and personal sketches which at least illustrate the growth and development of cartography as an art and as a science, during a period of about three centuries in which it has been built up to the threshold-line of modern scientific method.

This period was one of tentative effort, and of experimental and constructive growth, well worthy of attentive study.

During the past hundred years, art and method have become stereotyped, and the subjects for discussion in relation to map-structure have been narrowed down; though there yet remain problems of the representation of relief which can hardly be said to have been solved. For instance, representation pictorially on the flat surface of paper of mountainous or hilly areas remains even to-day of recognized difficulty, and the choice between contour lines and the layer system, and that of hachures, or vertical shading, results generally in something of a compromise and the adoption of both systems in part. This question is necessarily a critical one in such mountain areas as the Alps of Central Europe, and here it is to be noticed that the new Topographical Map of Switzerland is to be drawn in relief, with shading on the basis of light coming uniformly from the south, this being a departure from the method adopted in

the earliest modern large-scale map of the same country—
the *Carte Dufour*, upon which the light is shown as coming
from the north-west. The direction now to be adopted in
Switzerland for the conventional method of shading to
produce pictorial relief on the map surface seems to be
something of a reversion to the sixteenth century practice
of a westerly illumination, to which attention was drawn in
connection with the development of the cartographical art
at that time.

Such a comparison suggests one example of the co-
ordination and continuity of system throughout the whole
period which has been under consideration, and it justifies
concrete ideas of historical sequence in cartography, and the
study of the subject from this aspect, as one of considerable
importance.

Christopher Saxton, Nicolas Sanson, Alexis Hubert
Jaillot, César François Cassini de Thury, Joseph de Ferraris,
John Cary, William Roy, are the figures which, with their
associates and fellow-workers, may well stand out, and give
what one may call character-relief to a subject which might
otherwise appear dull and monotonous to the student. But
it can in truth, if properly handled, hardly be regarded as
a dull one. So treated it is alive with beauties—beauties of
art which appeal to the eye and to taste—beauties of science
and of human endeavour with which the whole structure is
adorned and illustrated, and it is from this point of view
that this book has been written and is now offered to the
public.

LIST OF WORKS OF REFERENCE

Box, Edward Gaspar. Lambarde's "Carde of this Shyre". (*Archaeologia Cantiana*, vol. XXXVIII.) *London*, 1926. 8º.

— Lambarde's "Carde of this Shyre". Third issue, with roads added. (*Archaeologia Cantiana*, vol. XXXIX.) *London*, 1928. 8º.

Cassini, César François. La Méridienne de l'Observatoire Royal de Paris, vérifiée dans toute l'étendue du Royaume par de Nouvelles Observations. *Paris*, 1744. 4º.

— Relation d'un Voyage en Allemagne, qui comprend les Opérations relatives à la Figure de la Terre et à la Géographie particulière du Palatinat, du Duché de Wurtemberg, du Cercle de Souabe, de la Bavière et de l'Autriche; fait par ordre du Roi. Suivie de la Description des Conquêtes de Louis XV, depuis 1745 jusqu'en 1748. *Paris*, 1775. 4º.

— Description Géométrique de la France. *Paris*, 1783. 4º.

Cassini, Jean Dominique. Voyage fait par ordre du Roi en 1768, pour éprouver les montres marines inventées par M. le Roy. *Paris*, 1770. 4º.

Chubb, Thomas. The Printed Maps of the Atlases of Great Britain and Ireland. A Bibliography, 1579–1870. With an Introduction by F. P. Sprent, and Biographical Notes on the Map Makers, Engravers and Publishers. *London*, 1927. 4º.

Close, Sir Charles. The Early Years of the Ordnance Survey. (*Royal Engineers Journal*.) *Chatham*, 1926. 8º.

Colby, Thomas. Ordnance Survey of the County of Londonderry. Memoir of the City and North-Western Liberties of Londonderry. Parish of Templemore. *Dublin*, 1837. 4º.

Drapeyron, Ludovic. Enquête à instituer sur l'exécution de la Grande Carte Topographique de France de Cassini de Thury. (*Revue de Géographie*, tome 38, Janvier–Juin, 1896.) *Paris*, 1896. 8º.

Ellis, Sir Henry. Speculi Britanniae Pars: An Historical and Chorographical Description of the County of Essex. By John Norden, 1594. Edited from the original Manuscript in the Marquess of Salisbury's Library at Hatfield, by Sir Henry Ellis. (*The Camden Society.*) *London*, 1840. 4°.

Fordham, Sir Herbert George. Studies in Carto-Bibliography, British and French, and in the Bibliography of Itineraries and Road-Books. *Oxford*, 1914. 8°.

— The Listes Générales des Postes de France, 1708–1779, and the Jaillots, géographes ordinaires du Roi. (*Transactions of the Bibliographical Society—The Library*—new series, vol. II.) *London*, 1922. 4°.

— John Ogilby (1600–1676). His *Britannia* and the British Itineraries of the eighteenth century. (*Transactions of the Bibliographical Society—The Library*—new series, vol. VI.) *London*, 1925. 4°.

— John Cary, Engraver, Map, Chart and Print-Seller and Globe-Maker, 1754 to 1835. A Bibliography, with an Introduction and Biographical Notes. *Cambridge*, 1925. 4°.

— Saxton's General Map of England and Wales. (*Geographical Journal*, vol. LXVII.) *London*, 1926. 8°.

— Une Carte-Routière de France du XVIIᵉ siècle. (*La Géographie*, Septembre–Octobre, 1926.) *Paris*, 1926. 8°.

— A Note on the "Quarter-Master's Map", 1644. (*Geographical Journal*, vol. LXX.) *London*, 1927. 8°.

— Some Surveys and Maps of the Elizabethan Period remaining in Manuscript. Saxton, Symonson and Norden. (*Geographical Journal*, vol. LXXII.) *London*, 1928. 8°.

— Christopher Saxton, of Dunningley, his Life and Work. (*Thoresby Society's Miscellanea*, vol. XXVIII.) *Leeds*, 1928. 8°.

Gerish, William Blyth. The Hertfordshire Historians. John Norden—1548–1626 (?)—a Biography. *Ware*, 1903. 8°.

Goblet d'Alviella, Le Comte Félix. Histoire des Bois et Forêts de Belgique. 3 tomes. *Paris and Brussels*, 1927. 8º.

Gould, Lt.-Commander Rupert T., R.N. The Marine Chronometer. Its History and Development. *London*, 1928. 8º.

Hannen, The Hon. Henry Arthur. An Account of a Map of Kent dated 1596. (*Archaeologia Cantiana*, vol. xxx.) *London*, 1913. 8º.

— Further Notes on Phil. Symonson, maker of a Map of Kent dated 1576–1596. (*Archaeologia Cantiana*, vol. xxxi.) *London*, 1915, 8º.

Hennequin, Lieut.-Colonel Émile. Étude Historique sur l'exécution de la Carte de Ferraris, et l'évolution de la cartographie en Belgique, depuis la publication de la carte de Flandre de Mercator (1540) jusque dans ces derniers temps. (*Bulletin de la Société Royale Belge de Géographie*, 1891.) *Brussels*, 1891. 8º.

Hinks, Arthur Robert. Maps and Survey. 2nd edition. *Cambridge*, 1922. 8º.

Laussedat, Colonel Aimé. Recherches sur les Instruments, les Méthodes et le Dessin Topographiques. 2 tomes. *Paris*, 1898–1903. 8º.

Le Roy, Pierre. Mémoire sur la meilleure manière de mesurer le temps en mer. (*Académie des Sciences*.) *Paris*, 1770.

Pollard, Alfred William. The Unity of John Norden: Surveyor and Religious Writer. (*Transactions of the Bibliographical Society—The Library—*new series, vol. vii.) *London*, 1926. 4º.

Reeves, Edward Ayearst. Maps and Map-Making. *London*, 1910. 8º.

Roland, Claude François. Alexis-Hubert Jaillot, Géographe du Roi Louis XIV (1632–1712). *Besançon*, 1919. 8º.

Roy, Major-General William. An Account of the Measurement of a Base on Hounslow Heath. (*Philosophical*

Transactions of the Royal Society, vol. LXXV.) *London*, 1785. 4°.

Roy, Major-General William. An Account of the Trigonometrical Operations, whereby the Distance between the Meridians of the Observatories of Greenwich and Paris has been determined. (*Philosophical Transactions of the Royal Society*, vol. LXXX.) *London*, 1790. 4°.

Taylor, Eva Germain Rimington. The Earliest Account of Triangulation. (*Scottish Geographical Magazine*, November, 1927.) *Edinburgh*, 1927. 8°.

— A Regional Map of the Early XVIth Century. (*Geographical Journal*, vol. LXXI.) *London*, 1928. 8°.

— William Bourne: A Chapter in Tudor Geography. (*Geographical Journal*, vol. LXXI.) *London*, 1928. 8°.

Vignon, E. J. M. Études Historiques sur l'Administration des Voies Publiques en France aux dix-septième et dix-huitième siècles. 3 tomes. *Paris*, 1862. 8°.

Supplementary volume. *Paris*, 1880. 8°.

Wolf, Charles. Histoire de l'Observatoire de Paris de sa fondation à 1793. *Paris*, 1902. 8°.

INDEX

Académie royale des Sciences, 31, 44 n., 46
Accuracy of triangulation, 42, 43
Actual Survey of the Great Post Roads between London and Falmouth (Cary), 55, 68, 72
Aix-la-Chapelle, Peace of, 49
Anciens Royaumes de Mercie et East-Angles, map of the, 25
Ancient Gaul, map of (Sanson), 24
Armorial Général de France, 30
Arrowsmith, Aaron, 72
Association founded by Cassini III, 38, 44 n., 50, 52, 53
Atlantic coast-lines, 21
Atlas (Lea), 8, 9; (Mercator), 21, 22; of the Counties of England and Wales (Saxton), 5; (Tassin), 29; (Web), 8; (Wildey), 9
Atlas Manuale, 19
Atlas Nouveau (Jaillot), 28–30, 33, 35, 38
Atlas Topographique et Militaire, 53
Atlas Universel, 32, 37, 38, 53
Austria, Emperor of, 62
Azores, St Mary in the, 6, 19

Bacon, Sir Francis, 14
Base, Dunkirk, 40; Hounslow Heath, 39, 40, 80, 81; Lough Foyle, 40, 43; Romney Marsh, 40, 81; Salisbury Plain, 40, 43
Bases in France, 40, 41
Benese, Sir Richarde de, 4
Berey, Jeanne, 29
Berey, Nicolas, 23, 29–31, 36

Bill, John, 18
Blagden, Dr Charles, 81, 82
Blakeney, William, Lord, 77
Boisseau, Jean, 23, 35
Boke of Measuryng of Lande, 4
Bouguereau, Maurice, 22, 23
Bowles, John & Son, 6
Bridges, on maps, 20; repair of, in Saxon times, 20
Britannia (Camden), 10, 15, 16; epitome of, 18
British Channel, chart of the (Cary), 70
British Isles, map of (Mercator), 8; triangulation of the, 44
Bulletin de la Société Royale Belge de Géographie, 67 n.
Burman Empire, map of (Cary), 74

Camden, William, 10, 15, 18
Camden Society, 12
Canary Islands, 19, 41
Canigou, 48
Capitaine, Louis, 54
Carde of this Shyre (Kent), 16
Cardiganshire, map of (Cary), 73
Carte de Cabinet (*Carte des provinces autrichiennes*), 36, 62–65; *mémoires* attached to, 64, 65
Carte de l'État Major (France), 53
Carte des Pays Conquis par le Roy, 49
Carte des Rivières de la France, 27

Carte Dufour, 87

Carte Geographicque des Postes qui traversent la France, 27

Carte Marchande (*Carte Chorographique des Pays-Bas Autrichiens*, 1777), 64

Cartes Générales de Toutes les Parties du Monde, 25, 26

Cartography, Dutch and Flemish school of, 24; French school of, 23, 24

Cartouches on maps, 37, 38

Cary, Francis, 69

Cary, George, 69

Cary, John, 7, 54, 55, 68–75, 75 n., 83, 87

Cary, William, 69, 75

Cassini, César François (III), 38, 42 n., 43, 44 n., 46–50, 52–56, 64, 68, 72, 78, 87; survey and triangulation in southern Germany, 55

Cassini, Jacques (II), 47, 48

Cassini, Jean Dominique (I), 31, 34, 46, 47

Cassini, Jean Dominique (IV), 47, 48, 53, 55, 78, 81, 82; imprisonment and trial, 47; voyage to Newfoundland, 55

Cassini family, 31, 39, 41, 46, 65, 76

Cassinis, publications of the, 55, 56

Charles IX, 23

Chronicles of England, Scotlande, and Irelande (Holinshed), 2

Chronometers of Le Roy, 55

Civil War in England, 7

Close, Sir Charles, 76, 77, 79, 82

Coast of France, table of principal places on the, 42 n.

Colbert, Jean Baptiste, 60

Colby, Major-General Thomas, 85

Colin, 30

College bursaries, estate maps in, 14

Colour on maps, 36, 37

Connection between observatories of Greenwich and Paris, 39, 40, 81, 82

Cordier, R., 25, 27

Cornwall, a description of (Norden), 10; the duchy of, surveys of manors, 13, 14

Coutans, Dom Guillaume, 60

Crown, surveyor to the, 9

Cruchley, George Frederick, 72, 74

Cumberland, Duke of, 76, 77

Dauphin, le Grand, 30, 30 n., 31, 48

Dee, Dr John, 9

Delineation of Northamptonshire, A (Norden), 10

Delisle, Guillaume, 33

Description des Conquêtes de Louis XV, 49

Description Géométrique de la France, 43, 44 n., 50, 56

Description of Britaine, The (Harrison), 2

Description of Cornwall, A Topographical and Chorographical (Norden), 10

Description of Hartfordshire, The (Norden), 10

Design and detail of maps, 19, 20, 21

Devonshire, map of (Donn), 73

Dewsbury, map of, 9

Digges, Leonard, 4

Distance Tables (Norden), 11

Donn, Benjamin, 73
Dover, visit of French surveyors to, 81, 82
Drapeyron, Ludovic, 46
Duchy of Cornwall, surveyor to the, 9
Dunkirk, 48
Dunkirk base, 40
Dupuis, L. A., 64

Early Years of the Ordnance Survey, The, 76
Elizabeth, Queen, 1, 2, 10
Elizabethan surveyors, 1–15
Ellis, Sir Henry, 10, 12
England, An Intended Guyde for English Travailers, 11
England, Wales, Scotland and Ireland Described, 18
England and Wales, county maps of (Saxton), 2, 3, 5, 8, 18; (Speed), 16; (Keer), 18; general map of (Lea), 6, 7, 28, 61; general map of (Saxton), 5–8, 28, 61; survey of, 2, 4, 5, 9
England and Wales with Part of Scotland (map) (Cary), 7, 54, 74
England and Wales and Part of Scotland (six-sheet map) (Cary), 74
English Atlas (Pitt), 22
Environs of London, map of (Cary and Wallis), 70
Essex, map of (Norden), 10; (Ordnance Survey), 84
Estate Surveys, 9, 12–14
Études Historiques sur l'Administration des Voies Publiques en France, 59
Europe, map of (Cary), 70

Faden, William, 42 n., 83, 84

Ferraris, Comte Joseph de, 36, 62–67, 66 n., 84, 87; life of, 65, 66, 66 n., 67 n.
Ferro, 19, 41
Feuillée, Louis, 41
Field of Mars, 70
Flamsteed, John, 46
Flanders, campaign in, 48, 49
Fontenoy, Battle of, 48
Forces de l'Europe, Asie, Afrique et Amérique, Les, 33
France, dimensions of, 31; map of (Capitaine), 54; (Cassini), 38, 43–46, 48, 50–55; (de La Guillotière), 23; (Ministry of War, Paris), 28, 61; (Postel), 23; maps of (Senex), 34; map of rivers, 27; road-maps of, 57–62; tables of places in, 42 n.; triangulation map of, 44 n., 48
French roads and bridges, plans and elevations of, 58–62
French school of cartography, art of, 35–38
French triangulation and survey, 41, 43, 44, 44 n., 45, 48

Garrett, John, 7
Gaul, map of ancient (Sanson), 24
Geographia (Ptolemy), 21
Geographical Journal, 4
Geological maps (William Smith), 74
Geological sections (William Smith), 74
George III, 40, 79
Germany, Cassini's surveys in southern, 55
Glamorganshire, map of (Cary), 73
Gough, Richard, 73

Greenwich, meridian of, 19
Greenwich Observatory, 39, 46, 79

Hampshire, map of (Norden), 10
Harrison, William, 2
Hartfordshire, The Description of, 10
Henry IV, 60
Hindostan, map of (Cary), 74
Histoire de l'Observatoire de Paris, 46
Hole, William, 15
Holinshed, Raphael, 2
Holland, Philemon, 10
Hollar, Wenceslaus, 7
Honour of Windsor, survey of, 12
Hounslow Heath base, 39, 40, 80, 81

Île de Fer, 19, 41
Illumination of maps, 35, 36
Improved Map of England and Wales (Cary), 74
Initial meridians, 6, 18, 19, 41
Intendants of the *Généralités* in France, 28, 58, 61
Introduction à l'Étude de la Géographie, 30
Ireland, memoirs of survey of, 84, 85
Isle of Man, map of, 6, 7

Jaillot, Alexis Hubert, 24, 29–36, 38, 87
Jaillot, Bernard Antoine, 32
Jaillot, Bernard Jean Hyacinthe, 32
Jaillot, Jean Baptiste Michel Renou de Chauvigné-, 32, 33
Jaillot, Simon, 29, 30
Jaillot family, 24, 29, 31, 32, 33

James I, 12
James II, 6
Jefferys, Thomas, 73
Jenner, Thomas, 7
John Cary, Engraver, Map, Chart and Print-Seller and Globe-Maker, 1754 to 1835, 75 n.
Joseph II, 66 n., 67 n.
Julien, Roch Joseph, 53

Keer, Peter, 17, 18
Keere, Pieter van den, 17, 18
Kent, map of (Faden-Ordnance Survey), 83, 84; (Symonson), 14
Kip, William, 15

La Guillotière, François de, 23
Lambarde, William, 14, 16
Langdon, Thomas, 14
Lea, Philip, 6, 8, 9, 61
Le Clerc, Jean, 23
Le Clerc, veuve Jean, 23
Legendre, Adrien Marie, 81
Le Roy, Pierre, 55
Liste Générale des Postes de France, 32
Lough Foyle base, 40, 43
Louis XIII, 19, 23
Louis XIV, 30, 30 n., 47
Louis XV, 48–52
Louis XVI, 60
Low Countries, conquest of, 48, 49; map of the (Ferraris), 36, 62–66

Man, Isle of, 6, 7
Manchester, map of, 9
Maps, astronomical method of construction, 42, 42 n., 43, 46; colour on, 36, 37; design and detail of, 19, 20, 21; illumination of, 35, 36; location of,

42; longevity of, 34; meridian of, 18, 19; orientation of, 18, 42; roads on, 6, 7, 20; scales on, 19; structure of, 42–44, 46
Maraldi, Giovanni Domenico, 42 n., 44 n.
Margarita Philosophica Nova (Reisch), 4
Mariette, Pierre, 23, 26, 27
Méchain, Pierre François André, 81
Mediterranean, coast-lines of, 21
Mercator, Gerhard, 8, 21, 22
Meridian of Azores, 19; of Canary Islands, 19; of Greenwich, 19; of London, 19; of maps, 18, 19; of St Paul's Cathedral, 19; on English maps, 19
Méridienne de l'Observatoire Royal de Paris vérifiée, La, 42 n., 56
Mews, Peter, Bishop of Winchester, 6
Middlesex, An historicall and chorographicall Description of, 10
Miscellanea (Thoresby Society), 4
Moll, Herman, 15, 19
Morden, Robert, 15
Morgan, William, 15, 20
Mortier, Pierre, 33, 35, 36
Mudge, Major-General William, 84

Namur, province of, map of the Crown Forests, 67
Neptune Français, Le, 31
New and Accurate Description (Paterson), 71
New and Correct English Atlas (Cary), 72
New English Atlas (Cary), 72

Newfoundland, voyage to (Cassini IV), 55
New Itinerary (Cary), 71
New Map of England and Wales with Part of Scotland (Cary), 7, 74
New Map of the County of Oxford (Cary), 73, 74
New Universal Atlas (Cary), 72
Norden, John, 1, 9–16, 20
Norden, John, junr., 12, 13
Norden's Description of Essex (Ellis), 12
Norden's Preparative to his Speculum Britanniae, 10
Norroy, King of Arms, 3
Northamptonshire, A Description of (Norden), 10
Nouvelle Carte qui comprend les principaux Triangles (France), 44 n., 45

Observatory, Royal, of Paris, 31, 39, 41, 46–48, 79; Royal, Greenwich, 39, 46, 79
Ogilby, John, 15, 20, 71; his survey of the roads of England and Wales, 20
Ordnance Survey, 40, 41, 44, 54, 65, 76, 78, 82–85; established, 40, 82; of Ireland, 84, 85
Orientation of maps, 18, 42
Ortelius, Abraham, 2, 21, 22, 35
Oxfordshire, map of (Cary), 73, 74

Palmer, William, 69
Paris, Royal Observatory of, 31, 39, 41, 46–48, 79
Paterson, Daniel, 71
Pathway to Patience in all Manner of Afflictions, 11
Pensive Man's Practise, A, 11

Perambulation of Kent, A (Lambarde), 14, 16
Petit Neptune Français, 42 n.
Peyrounin, A., 27
Philosophical Transactions (Royal Society), 76
Pitt, Moses, 22
Plane-table, 4, 79
Planisphere (Cassini's), 34; of places in France, 47
Plantin, Christopher, 8
Polymetrum (Waldseemüller), 4
Ponts et Chaussées, department of the, 37, 58–60
Portolan charts, 21
Postel, Guillaume, 23
Post-roads of France, maps of the, 27, 32
Preparative to his Speculum Britanniae, Norden's, 10
Projet et Acte d'Association (Cassini's), 44 n., 52, 53
Ptolemy (Claudius Ptolemaeus), 21, 31

Quartermaster's Map (Hollar), 7, 20

Ramsden, Jesse, 40, 69, 80
Ramsden's theodolite, 40
Rebellion in Scotland in 1745, 76, 77
Regional Survey, 65, 84
Reisch, Gregorius, 4
Relation d'un Voyage en Allemagne, 49
Reports of the Intendants on the roads of France, 28, 61
Richelieu, Cardinal de, 19, 41
Rivers of France, map of the, 27
Roads of France, maps of the, 27, 28, 37, 58–62
Robert de Vaugondy, Didier, 24, 31, 37, 53

Robert de Vaugondy, Gilles, 24, 31, 37, 53
Rochester Bridge estate, 14
Rocque, John, 7
Romney Marsh base, 40, 81
Route de Paris à Reims (Coutans), 60
Roy, Major-General William, 39, 40, 76–82, 87
Royal Society, Philosophical Transactions of the, 76
Russia, map of (Cary), 74

Salisbury Plain base, 40, 43
Sanson, Adrien, 24, 26, 28, 30
Sanson, Guillaume, 24, 26, 28, 30
Sanson, Nicolas, 22–30, 34, 38, 48, 87
Sanson, Nicolas, jun., 24
Sanson family, 31
Sansons' smaller atlases, 28
Saxton, Christopher, 1–9, 11, 15–21, 34, 61, 72, 87; general map of England and Wales, 5–8, 61; grant of armorial bearings to, 3; grant of Grigston Manor to, 3; grant of land in the parish of St Sepulchre without Newgate to, 3; grant of reversion to receivership of the Hospital of St John of Jerusalem in England to, 3; letter for survey in Wales, 4, 5; licence to publish maps, 2, 3; private survey maps, 9; maps of the counties of England and Wales, 2, 3, 5, 8, 9
Sayer, Robert, 7
Scales on maps, 19
Scotland, rebellion in (1745), 76, 77
Seckford, Thomas, 2, 6, 9

Seller, John, 15, 19, 20
Senex, John, 15, 34
Ships on maps, time of Elizabeth, 6; time of James II, 6
Somer, Jean, 27
Sommer, Jean, 27
Speed, John, 16, 18, 34
Smith, William, 74
Stanhope, Sir Michael, 13; survey of his estate, 13
Stent, Peter, 8
Structure of maps, 42–44, 46
Sully, Duc de, 60
Surrey, map of (Norden), 10
Survey, instruments of, 4, 39, 40; of France, royal order for, 49, 50; systems of, 4
Surveyors Dialogue, 10
Sussex, map of, 73; map of (Norden), 10
Symonson, Philip, 14, 20

Table alphabétique des lieux, 42 n.
Tables of places on the coast of France, 42 n.
Tassin, Nicolas, 23, 29
Tavernier, Gabriel, 22
Tavernier, Melchior, 23, 27, 28
Taylor, Miss E. G. R., 4
Templemore, parish of, memoir (Ordnance Survey of Ireland), 84, 85
Théâtre François (Bouguereau), 22
Theatre of the Empire of Great Britaine, 16

Theatrum Orbis Terrarum (Ortelius), 22
Theodolite of Leonard Digges, 4; of Jesse Ramsden, 40, 81
Traveller's Companion (Cary), 72
Triangulation, 4, 39–46, 44 n., 48, 49, 79–82; accuracy of, 42, 43; in south of England (Roy), 79–82; of British Isles, 44; of France, map of, 43–45, 44 n.
Turgot, Anne Robert Jacques, 58

Vauban, Sébastien Le Prestre, Maréchal de, 33
Vienna Foreign Office, 63
Vignon, E. J. M., 59
Voltaire, on roads of Europe, 63
Voyage to Newfoundland (Cassini IV), 55

Waldseemüller, Martin, 4
Wales, Henry, Prince of, 12
Wales, survey of, 4, 5
Wallis, John, 70
Watson, Lieut.-General, 77, 79
Web, William, 8
Whitwell, Charles, 10
Wildey, George, 9
Windsor, 12
Windsor Castle, 12
Wolf, Charles, 46
Wood MSS., Bodleian Library, 3
World-map, 19

For EU product safety concerns, contact us at Calle de José Abascal, 56–1°, 28003 Madrid, Spain or eugpsr@cambridge.org.

www.ingramcontent.com/pod-product-compliance
Ingram Content Group UK Ltd.
Pitfield, Milton Keynes, MK11 3LW, UK
UKHW012334130625
459647UK00009B/279